M000207546

Praise for *Remei*

The church needs to explore baptism. _____
vital connection to genuine Christian discipleship that is ever-oriented toward both fellowship and mission. In this book, Meadows keeps one eye on the early church and the Methodist movement as rich resources and guides, and the other eye on the challenging, even perplexing, context of a post-Christian, often hostile culture. What emerges from such labor is a deftly written and engaging account, punctuated by crisp personal narrative, that like Christian discipleship itself is nothing less than a joy.

Dr. Kenneth J. Collins, Professor of Historical Theology and Wesley Studies, Asbury Theological Seminary

This is a timely, much-needed book. Meadows offers a "big and living" understanding of Christian baptism, expertly weaving together biblical and Wesleyan themes into a challenging but deeply attractive pattern. The result is a "must read" for those desiring to be better Christian disciples today and particularly those of us belonging to congregations seeking new purpose and direction.

Rev. Dr. Martyn Atkins, Westminster Central Hall, and former General Secretary of the Methodist Church in Great Britain

Meadows has written a serious challenge to the church that is accessible to a broad readership. He convincingly shows how living out the sacrament of baptism fundamentally entails committed discipleship, the pursuit of holy living, engagement in God's mission, and participation in a community of disciple makers. These four marks of an authentic Christian and distinctively Wesleyan way of life set the context for any fruitful discussion of the proper age for baptism, or the purpose of confirmation, or the relationship of baptism to evangelical conversion experience. Each chapter concludes with a set of discussion questions for further reflection, which makes this an ideal resource for small-group study. But what is most compelling is the way Meadows keeps pushing his readers to reconsider how their own baptism is a lifelong journey to grow more deeply in the love of God, through Jesus Christ, by the power of the Holy Spirit. I recommend this book heartily, and I plan to use it in my own congregation.

Dr. L. Edward Phillips, Associate Professor of Worship and Liturgical Theology, Emory University

Jesus left his disciples a mission to go into the world baptizing and teaching. Philip Meadows's Remembering Our Baptism *provides the teaching to understand baptism as the church's mission. He does so in a distinctly Wesleyan key, which means it is catholic mixed with Anabaptism, drawing upon holiness traditions. This book should be read in every seminary and local church to help Wesleyans in particular, and Christians in general, to understand what it means to grow into their baptisms. More importantly, it should be required study for every clergy person so that he or she might understand the sacred gift entrusted to them in baptizing and calling the faithful to remember their baptism.*

Dr. D. Stephen Long, Cary M. Maguire University Professor of Ethics, Southern Methodist University

Remembering Our Baptism *aims to awaken twenty-first century Christians from a trance: an oppressive spiritual amnesia, in which we have forgotten that to be baptized is to be committed to a lifelong pursuit of holiness. Not only does it prod us again and again to recall the logic of our calling, but it is also a workbook to help readers live as those committed to the obedience that alone renews and transforms. We are challenged to "live wet" and given practical help to do so. This is a book rooted in the Wesleyan heritage of its writer, but one that offers a timely, rigorous but encouraging word to all those seeking to follow the way of Jesus.*

Dr. Peter Hatton, Coordinator of Theological Education, Bristol Baptist College (UK)

The baptismal covenant shapes the mission of every United Methodist congregation as it strives to make disciples of Jesus Christ for the transformation of the world. Phil Meadows provides a powerful and practical resource to help people understand how baptism, discipleship, and mission are connected. Remembering Our Baptism *will help the people of The United Methodist Church claim their identity as citizens of God's kingdom, centered in the life and mission of Jesus Christ in the world.*

Dr. Steve Manskar, Director of Wesleyan Leadership, Discipleship Ministries, United Methodist Church

Phil Meadows's passionate commitment to discipleship comes through in this book. Don't be fooled; it's about baptism for sure, but as a way into profound discipleship. The book is rife with deep, provocative, insightful questions to stimulate discussion, touching heart, mind, and soul. The advocacy for a kind of Christian discipleship rooted in Christian community and thoughtfully engaged with the very best of the Wesleyan heritage is inspirational. Many of the challenges of current church life are named and responded to. I highly commend this book for its practical wisdom and its author for living it out. The church needs to absorb, embrace, and commit to discipleship now more than ever, and this accessible book will help that endeavor.

Dr. Deirdre Brower-Latz, Principal, Nazarene Theological College, Didsbury, Manchester (UK)

Phil Meadows helps us make important connections between baptism, discipleship, and mission. He continually points to a holistic understanding that encompasses all aspects of the Christian life. Following Jesus means "living wet," and he challenges us to live more fully devoted to Christ.

Bishop Scott J. Jones, Houston Episcopal Area, United Methodist Church

Phil Meadows writes with clarity and persuasion, which comes from a mixture of profound theology and missional passion. By linking mission and baptism through discipleship, he gives us the freedom to re-examine the very purpose of baptism without tiresome contentious descent into details of its practices. Though the book is unashamedly Wesleyan, it will be read with profit by all those who baptize infants or believers. There are increasing numbers of books on discipleship; this one takes a fresh route through the waters of baptism.

Rev. Dr. George Lings, former Director of Research, Church Army, Wilson Carlile Centre (UK)

After two thousand years, Christians still ask, "What does it mean to live in light of our baptism?" Meadows demonstrates in this book that what we need today are not new liturgies for Remembering Our Baptism, *but rather renewed patterns of discipleship that facilitate a living of our baptism today. Serious seekers of life in Christ will find this book a helpful tool as they mature as disciples of Jesus.*

Dr. Jack Jackson, E. Stanley Jones Associate Professor of Evangelism, Mission, and Global Methodism, Claremont School of Theology

Meadows is determined to help readers "live wet" by reflecting on the connections between baptism, discipleship, and mission. He focuses on the kind of life into which Christians are baptized—we must remember how to live because of whose we now are, becoming more like Jesus in mind, heart, and life. Jesus started a disciple-making movement to save the whole world. A proper extension of his ministry is seen in the early Methodist movement, a disciple-making movement of "real" Christians seeking a holy existence in love with God and neighbor. Designed as an ideal text for the classroom or small-group study, this valuable resource is for all believers wanting to actually "live wet" the mission implications of their baptisms.

Dr. Barry Callen, longtime Editor of the *Wesleyan Theological Journal*, currently Editor of Aldersgate Press and Secretary of the Wesleyan Holiness Connection and Horizon International

I will confess that an approach to the topic of discipleship and mission in the Wesleyan tradition through the lens of baptism was a surprise at first! However, the biblical, theological, and practical reflection into which Phil Meadows leads us presents a deep challenge to contemporary Methodism, and creates a longing that we might "remember who we are." The fact that Meadows brings a depth of academic research and reflection, years of Christian discipleship, and a deep passion for God to this topic is evident again and again throughout this book. The Irish Methodist Church is proud to count Phil as one of our number! God has blessed us through his ministry, and I am sure that God will bless, challenge, and encourage many as this book is read and discussed.

Rev. Dr. Heather Morris, Home Mission Secretary, Methodist Church in Ireland

REMEMBERING OUR BAPTISM

Discipleship and Mission
in the Wesleyan Spirit

PHILIP R. MEADOWS

DISCIPLESHIP
RESOURCES

ISBN 978-0-88177-888-5
Scripture quotations are from the New International Version unless otherwise stated.
Holy Bible, New International Version®, NIV® Copyright ©1973, 1978, 1984, 2011 by Biblica, Inc.® Used by permission. All rights reserved worldwide.

DR888

DEDICATION

This book is dedicated to my mother, Margaret Meadows, and to my late father, Harold. They baptized me as a child and have unconditionally loved me, believed in me, encouraged me, taken pride in me, and supported me throughout my life. In baptism, they dedicated me to God. In parenting, they became co-workers with his prevenient grace, knowingly and unknowingly, through thick and thin. In later years, they supported my missionary calling so I might "live wet," even when it cost them to do so. Mum and Dad, you have fulfilled your baptismal vows over me and enabled me to know the joy of discipleship.

ABOUT THE COVER

The cover artwork for this book was designed and created by Timothy Meadows, son of the author. The image depicts what it means to "live wet" as a baptized follower of Jesus. It weaves together the main themes of the book: baptism as an initiation into the life of discipleship; a dedication to the pursuit of Christ-likeness; a participation in the mission of God; and a collaboration in disciple-making fellowship. Remembering our baptism is about taking up this vocation and discovering the joy of following Jesus as a community of everyday missionaries.

CONTENTS

ACKNOWLEDGMENTS

I am forever indebted to my wife, Samantha, for her patient love and co-working in the gospel. She is the finest example of what it means to be a baptized follower of Jesus, and she has always put flesh on the ideas we have shared in this book. I am thankful for the understanding of my children, Daniel, Tabitha, Timothy, and Benjamin, who have supported me every day with their prayers, even as I have disappeared into my study. I have benefited from the many students in my classes on Wesleyan studies, evangelism, and mission, who have helped me hone the ideas in this book over many years. But I am especially grateful for my research students, Jack Jackson, Brian Yeich, David Hull, Tammie Grimm, and Lorna Koskela, who also gave substantive feedback on the manuscript, and it is so much better for it. I am thankful to my friend Steve Manskar in Discipleship Ministries (United Methodist Church), who saw the potential in this project and has encouraged me to see it through. Finally, I recognize the importance of my church family in helping to shape my vision of baptism. They have been up to their waists in warm water when baptizing my children and up to their necks in hot water when wrestling with me over what it all means. I have been so blessed by the spiritual friendship of Jim Bawden and Ian Hardwick, who have helped me to remember my baptism on a weekly basis for many years in our fellowship band.

FOREWORD

Remembering Our Baptism is a soul-searching book, timely and much-needed. It offers a way to take seriously—to actually practice—what people pledge in their Christian baptism, and what the congregation itself promises. Phil Meadows calls the book "an exercise in holding on to the doctrine, spirit, and discipline of the early Methodist movement, through the practice of remembering our baptism." The language of "remembering baptism" as presented here means much more, of course, than mere remembering as a cognitive function. Not just an act of memory, but a move into commitment and day-by-day discipleship in Christian community. Not just recalling to mind, but rather entering into true Christian vocation. This is the kind of remembering the Bible itself calls for: Remembering our covenant with God so that we actually walk in God's ways.

Several recent books—most pointedly perhaps Alan Kreider's *The Patient Ferment of the Early Church*—have analyzed the amazing dynamism of early Christianity. Also, within the Methodist tradition, a number of authors are calling for the renewal of the Wesleyan witness and exploring ways this could happen. Meadows's book goes deeper, analyzing Methodism's DNA in light of what we are learning about the genes and genius of the earliest Christian communities in their practice of discipleship and mission. So this book focuses on "baptism as an initiation into the life of discipleship and a participation in the mission of God." Baptism should be not just a public profession of faith but must involve "embarking on a journey of discipleship that requires us to deny ourselves and take up our cross daily as lifelong and whole-life followers of Jesus." This certainly was true in the early church, and in fact whenever the church has been a dynamic movement changing people's lives and molding society. Meadows shows how the early church's central focus on discipleship—that is, faithful Christian living in the world—got diluted during and after the time of the Emperor Constantine, as well as the inadequacy of confirmation as generally practiced today. But the church can recover much of the dynamic of the early Christian catechumenate through practices that help believers turn their baptism into a life pattern.

The book proposes a "remembering" process involving four key elements: (1) initiation into the life of discipleship, (2) dedication to the pursuit of holiness, (3) participation in the mission of God, and (4) collaboration in disciple-making fellowships involving covenant groups. Through these, Meadows believes, churches today can recover—or better, experience for themselves—the life-changing dynamic of early Methodism and of real Christianity at its best.

Meadows does not focus on the *mode* of baptism, but on its meaning and ongoing relevance for Christian life. He deals forthrightly with the problems posed by infant baptism and confirmation in the case of people who have never really experienced life-transforming grace in their lives. Picking up on the heart of John Wesley's practice, Meadows argues that "those who experience the new birth should be incorporated into something like band meetings, as the primary mark of a baptized disciple." How to do this practically is the heart of the book.

Discussing Wesley's much misunderstood term "social holiness," Meadows rightly says that "the *social* nature of holiness means our discipleship must be worked out in the company and conversation of others" in a process of "gathering and scattering."

His extended discussion of social holiness restores this important Wesleyan emphasis to the full dynamic that Wesley intended.

Meadows insists the meaning of the Great Commission "is not merely to pass on the gospel of the kingdom by any available means but to pass on the very life of the kingdom by the methods that Jesus used." The word "teaching" in the Great Commission means not just "informing people about the message of the kingdom, but imparting to people the life of the kingdom." If baptism truly means conversion, Meadows says, it involves "not merely a change of heart but a transformation of one's whole life." This is what we find in the early church, where evangelism took considerable time. Disciple making "was not just one activity among many, but the organizing center of its life and worship, as a community of mission." The point is, the same can be true today.

Meadows is on target when he says "salvation and discipleship is about being caught up in God's ultimate purposes for the renewal of all creation." The relevance of true Christian discipleship for the renewal of creation, including the Christian responsibility of creation care today, is urgent. If we Christians are not only to build the church but properly steward God's garden, we will have to learn deep discipleship.

Although this book will be useful across a broad spectrum theologically and denominationally, it is particularly rich in its use of Wesleyan sources, including Charles Wesley's hymns. The book should be especially helpful to baptized believers who intend to take their faith seriously, or who are sincerely wondering what the discipleship implications of the gospel they profess really are for daily life in today's world.

—Howard A. Snyder, former Professor of the History and Theology of Mission, Asbury Theological Seminary

REFERENCES AND ABBREVIATIONS

Bible   All citations are from the New International Version unless otherwise stated.
Holy Bible, New International Version®, NIV® Copyright ©1973, 1978, 1984, 2011 by Biblica, Inc.® Used by permission. All rights reserved worldwide.

WJW   Thomas Jackson (Ed.), *The Works of John Wesley* (1872), 14 Volumes. A good resource for Wesley's works online, http://wesley.nnu.edu/john-wesley/.

Covenant   General Board of Discipleship, *A Collection of the Services of the Baptismal Covenant in the United Methodist Church* (United Methodist Publishing House, 2009), https://www.umc discipleship.org/resources/a-collection-of-the-services-of-the-baptismal-covenant-revised-2008.

Hymns   John Wesley (Ed.), *A Collection of Hymns for the People Called Methodists* (1780).

Journal   Journal entry by John Wesley, in WJW.

Letter   Letter from John Wesley, in WJW.

Lives	Thomas Jackson (Ed.), *The Lives of Early Methodist Preachers*, 5th Edition (Wesleyan-Methodist Book Room, 1865).
Minutes	Thomas Jackson (Ed.), *Minutes of Several Conversations* (1797).
Notes	John Wesley, *Explanatory Notes Upon the New Testament* (Epworth Press, 1977).
People	John Wesley, "A Plain Account of the People Called Methodists," in WJW 8:263–286.
Prayers	John Wesley, "A Collection of Prayers for Every Day of the Week," in WJW 11:232–277.
Rules	John Wesley, "The Nature, Design and General Rules of the United Societies," in WJW 8:287–289.
Sermon	Sermon by John Wesley, in WJW.
Spirituality	Paul Chilcote, *Early Methodist Spirituality: Selected Women's Writings* (Kingswood Books, 2007).
Treatise	John Wesley, "A Treatise Upon Baptism," in WJW 10:203–215.

Introduction

Like any means of grace, baptism is a means to an end, not an end in itself. As we shall see, turning the means into an end is the quickest way to undermine its real meaning and purpose. So, despite the title of this book, our main concern will not be the practice of baptism as such. Questions about who, when, and how we baptize are critical, but this is not where we start. The first questions are: "What are we doing when we baptize? And what kind of life are we baptized into?"

One outcome of liturgical renewal among Methodists and many other church traditions has been to recover the continuing significance of baptism (often from infancy) throughout the Christian life.[1] As a result, there has been much theological reflection on "renewing," "reaffirming," or "remembering" our baptism, and resources have been produced for engaging this conversation in the church.[2] Again, the real value of these practices depends on what is being remembered and what difference it makes in our lives.

Our starting point lies in the subtitle of the book: "Discipleship and Mission in the Wesleyan Spirit." Remembering our baptism should cause us to wrestle with what it means to participate in the mission of God. So, the question that will shape our thinking is this: "What has baptism got to do with mission?" Or, to put it the other way around, "What does mission look like from the perspective of baptism?" And I will try to explain why the answer to both questions is, "Discipleship."

THE PROBLEM OF CHEAP GRACE

The theology and practice of Martin Luther has been a major influence on the idea of remembering our baptism. Through the course of the Reformation, he often came face to face with the demonic powers of fear and death, both in the church and the world. In the midst of great discouragement, he felt tempted to doubt the promises of God and give up his work. At such times, Luther would splash water on himself and shout at his demons, "I am baptized!" He did not say, "I *have been* baptized," but "I *am* baptized." Baptism is a matter of identity and vocation.

This reminds us of what happened when Jesus was baptized at the outset of his ministry. After the Spirit had descended upon him, many witnesses heard God's voice declaring Jesus to be his beloved Son. Strengthened by those words of assurance, Jesus resisted the temptation to compromise in the wilderness and the temptation to quit in the garden by remembering who he was. The grand strategy of the powers of evil to undermine the work of God among his people has always been tempting them to forget who and whose they are. And our Spirit-empowered response to this temptation has always been the same, to remember our baptism and thus reaffirm our identity. The life of discipleship flows from knowing that we are children of the living God and remembering that our identity was given to us in baptism. This is true for individuals and for the whole community of baptized disciples as the family of God.

Luther's practice of remembrance was deeply shaped by his own theological convictions about the nature of baptism.[3] First, he thought of baptism as a sign that we are made right with God by grace and faith alone. We have done nothing to deserve being called the children of God, and so we remember his unconditional love toward us. Second, baptism is a sign that we have been clothed in Christ, not a righteousness of our own. When God looks upon us, he sees Christ in our place, and we are assured of his forgiveness no matter what. Third, baptism is a sign that God is utterly faithful and will never give up on us. No matter how much we stumble and fall, his steadfast love endures forever, and our new life in him can never be lost.

While there is much to celebrate in these profound truths, there is also a danger lurking beneath the surface. If our salvation rests on nothing more than God's unconditional love and grace, then there is nothing to gain or lose in the life of discipleship. Wesley himself realized how this leaves us one step away from merely celebrating the forgiveness of sins but abandoning the pursuit of holiness. Dietrich Bonhoeffer lamented this problem in his own Lutheran tradition and named it "cheap grace," which he said was "the deadly enemy of our church." He argued, "We are fighting today for costly grace."[4]

Although Luther probably would not condone cheap grace, it seems that his theology does not go far enough to prevent it. The great danger is that we might turn the act of remembering our baptism into a practice of cheap grace by seeking to renew our identity in Christ while refusing to grow up in his likeness. We are tempted to settle for the reassurance of being called the children of God without the responsibility of walking worthy of our vocation.

REMEMBRANCE IN THE WESLEYAN SPIRIT

John Wesley's thoughts on baptism clearly reflect his orienting concerns as leader of an evangelical renewal movement within the Church of England.[5] As an Anglican priest, he upheld the practice of infant baptism, repeating the received wisdom of the church with little adaptation (including the idea of infant regeneration or new birth).[6] He wasted no time in recording any original theological reflection on the nature of baptism that might have yielded a specifically Wesleyan doctrine for the Methodist movement. We can say with certainty, however, that Wesley considered the sacrament to be effective in preparing people for Christian discipleship through incorporation into the church.

Although we do not have much unambiguous access to Wesley's thoughts on baptism, his descriptions of discipleship and fellowship are abundant. If remembering our baptism is meant to shape a whole way of life, as Luther has suggested, then it should be possible to pursue a more Wesleyan approach on that basis. In other words, we might examine what lies at the heart of Wesleyan spirituality and examine the extent to which it is baptismal in shape.

Central to the argument of this book, then, is the suggestion that we need to go beyond striving for more adequate liturgies of remembering our baptism. Rather, we need to recover the meaning of baptism as a call to "live wet" as a baptized follower of Jesus in the practices of whole-life and lifelong discipleship.[7] This will mean moving our attention away from periodic acts of remembrance during baptism itself, or in confirmation, or at other formal services of baptismal affirmation. Rather, we will focus on the practices of discipleship and fellowship in the early Methodist movement to explore how they embody a baptismal way of life. More than that, our aim is to explore the connections between baptism, discipleship, and mission. Turning to Wesley for clues about the contemporary meaning of baptism is promising because of what we can learn from early Methodism as a disciple-making movement on mission with God.

TAKING WESLEY AS A MENTOR

Wesley was determined to become a "real" and "altogether" Christian, holy in heart and life, perfected in love of God and neighbor.[8] This vision was cultivated and pursued through his encounters with, and appropriation of, many different streams of Christian thought and practice. He drew upon early church writers from both East and West: Anglican divines, Puritans and Pietists, Moravians, and even heretics! In short, he "poached" anything that could help illumine the life of discipleship as the pursuit of holiness. One might say that he was a theological mongrel.

My own journey of faith has also been complicated. I was evangelized by Pentecostals, brought to faith by evangelical Anglicans, taught the mysteries by high-church priests, encouraged by parachurch ministries, befriended by independent church leaders, filled with the Spirit in charismatic worship, learned to preach under the tutelage of Methodists, married into a Baptist family, trained at a British Methodist theological college, worked at a United Methodist Seminary in the USA, participated in a Free Methodist church and an American Baptist church, started a house fellowship, and I am now in full connection with the Methodist Church in Ireland! If being a theological mongrel is what it takes to become a fully devoted follower of Jesus, then I am with Wesley!

In this book, I will focus on the writing of Wesley and the example of the early Methodist movement, while making connections to the practice of baptism in the contemporary church. To facilitate this, I begin each chapter with a reference to the baptismal liturgy of The United Methodist Church, insofar as it contains themes that are common to most Wesleyan traditions. But like Wesley, I will also "poach" upon a variety of other traditions and spiritual movements insofar as they help to illuminate a specifically Wesleyan theology of baptism, discipleship, and mission. In most cases, I will simply be tracing the influences on Wesley himself and the clues he left for us to follow.

MAPPING THE WAY FORWARD

In chapter 1, we make the Great Commission our starting point and use it to trace the scriptural connections between baptism, discipleship, and mission. We examine the baptism of Jesus and how that shaped his own way of life as a participant in the mission of God. This helps us see how he gathered a community of baptized disciples, trained them to baptize others, and then sent them out to make disciples of all nations. Although Wesley does not use the term "disciple" or "discipleship" very often, the business of making disciples was at the heart of the movement he founded. Remembering our baptism means reflecting on the commission to be disciple-making communities on mission with God.

Chapter 2 develops the idea that baptism sends us all out as ordinary missionaries in the context of our daily lives. A missionary is literally someone who is "sent," and we will see that all discipleship should be missional in nature. We will reflect briefly on the origin of modern missions in the Puritan, Pietist, and Revival movements and their influences on early Methodism. In particular, they highlight the costly nature of fulfilling the commission to make disciples. Remembering our baptism means grappling with the idea that the Great Commission is for everyone and confronting some reasons why we fail to be disciple-making communities.

In chapter 3, we look at baptism in the name of the Father, Son, and Spirit as an immersion into life-giving fellowship with the triune God. This helps us interpret the way of salvation in Wesley's theology as a journey of discipleship through conversion and holiness. Discipleship as a way of salvation means being transformed into the likeness of Jesus by the indwelling power of his Spirit from the inside out. Remembering our baptism means becoming co-workers with God in our own journey of discipleship and by inviting others to make the journey themselves.

Chapter 4 delves more deeply into the meaning of baptism as a sign of conversion. This draws our attention to the general state of discipleship in the Church of England during the eighteenth century and the problem of nominal Christianity. The early Methodist movement created a paradox in the meaning of conversion by calling those who had already been baptized as infants to the experience of new birth. Remembering our baptism means facing our perpetual need for true conversion, renewal, and revitalization, both as individuals and communities of discipleship.

In chapter 5, we consider the nature of baptism as a mark of being in covenant relationship with God. Covenant renewal in the Scripture is a way of overcoming the problem of spiritual amnesia, or forgetting our true identity and vocation as disciples. Renewing our covenant with God became a distinctive practice in early Methodism, which Wesley adapted from the Puritan tradition of the previous century. Wesley explicitly described this in terms of the baptismal covenant and as a means of repentance, conversion, and commitment to Jesus as Savior and Lord. Remembering our baptism means refusing to forget who we are by accepting the invitation to take up our cross daily and follow Jesus in discipleship and mission.

Chapter 6 begins to explore why baptism should be the heartbeat of a missional community. Wesley left us some explicit clues about the similarity between the disciple-making practices of Methodist society and the early church catechumenate. This helps us explore how the early Methodist movement, which emerged in the depths of Christendom, can illumine a way forward for evangelistic mission in our own post-Christendom culture. Remembering our baptism means learning how to live as an attractive witness to the gospel in a culture that is increasingly hostile to real Christianity.

In chapter 7, we develop the theme of witness in a hostile culture by examining how baptism plunges us into a life of spiritual warfare. We do this by unpacking the baptismal vows to renounce, reject, and resist the spiritual forces of evil, both within our own hearts and in the world at large. In particular, we see how fighting the good fight is not something we can do on our own. This helps to explain Wesley's famous claim that there is no such thing as solitary Christianity. The early Methodist movement was organized to beat the devil and set people free from the powers of worldliness for the pursuit of holiness. Remembering our baptism means accepting that we must fight or die, and the only way to live is through collaboration in the discipline of Christian fellowship.

Chapter 8 opens up the meaning of baptism as incorporation into the church and its call to be a disciple-making community. This causes us to reflect on the vows made by the church to nurture the life and witness of its members. There are clear parallels between the early Methodist movement and the disciple-making emphases of radical Christianity exemplified in the Anabaptist tradition. By making this comparison, we see how Wesley's theology of social holiness provides a key to understanding the visible witness of the church, both gathered in its life together and scattered in the everyday lives of faithful disciples. Remembering our baptism means creating a discipleship culture in the church that raises up authentic followers of Jesus.

In chapter 9, we turn to the thorny topic of baptism and being filled with the Spirit. We explore why this is the necessary power for growing in discipleship and living as effective witnesses in the world. The early Methodist movement emerged in the context of revival, so we tease out the pervading influence of revival spirituality on its practices of discipleship and mission. We will see how the gift of the Spirit is essential for the pursuit of holiness and how the Spirit-filled life is nurtured in a Spirit-filled community of disciples. Remembering our baptism means acknowledging our power failure and waiting together for the gift of the Spirit to revive our discipleship and reboot our missionary witness.

Chapter 10 draws together the different themes of the book, offers a few simple reflections on how remembering our baptism might be put into practice today, and presents the possibility of renewing the church as a disciple-making movement.

How to Read This Book

Although the book takes the reader on a journey of exploration, each chapter is a topic in its own right. I have added a question for reflection at the beginning that captures the overarching theme. I have also concluded each chapter with a summary of how to remember our baptism in light of each topic, together with some further questions for self-examination and group discussion. The best way to study the material is in relatively small groups of around five people who will work through the book one chapter at a time. The benefit of such groups is that they are small enough to reflect on the material deeply and encourage one another to practice what is being learned in their daily lives. Ideally, each participant will read and reflect on the material before coming to the next meeting. The group members will then practice remembering their baptism by sharing how they have been comforted and challenged by what they have read. Finally, group members should take time to acknowledge how the Spirit may be leading them forward and resolve to follow through with the support and prayers of the group. Above all, let us remember who we are and whose we are, and count the cost of discipleship and mission. Why? Because "discipleship is joy!"[9]

CHAPTER 1

The Great Commission

Eternal Father . . . In the fullness of time you sent Jesus . . . He was baptized by John and anointed by your Spirit. He called his disciples to share in the baptism of his death and resurrection and to make disciples of all nations.[1]

Remembering our baptism means hearing the Great Commission as a personal command to be a disciple who makes disciples. Are you living as a mission-shaped disciple who helps other people meet Jesus and grow in their discipleship?

When someone is baptized, it presents the whole church with an opportunity to thank God for sending Jesus and to remember that Jesus now sends us to share in his ministry of making disciples. In other words, being a missionary (someone who is "sent") is essential to the very nature of discipleship. So, we start our reflections on the connection between baptism, discipleship, and mission with the Great Commission in Matthew's Gospel:

Then the eleven disciples went to Galilee, to the mountain where Jesus had told them to go. When they saw him, they worshiped him; but some doubted. Then Jesus came to them and said, "All authority in heaven and on earth has been given to me. Therefore go and make disciples of all nations, baptizing them in the name of the Father and of the Son and of the Holy Spirit, and teaching them to obey everything I have commanded you. And surely I am with you always, to the very end of the age" (Mt 28:16-20).

The main verb, which encompasses the whole meaning of this text, is the command to "make disciples." As Wesley put it, this is "the whole design of Christ's commission."[2] These are the parting words of the risen Jesus to his community of disciples, so they have often been taken as a summary of the church's vocation in the world. For example, United Methodists explain, "The mission of the Church is to make disciples of Jesus Christ."[3] The Methodist Church in Ireland claims, "the flourishing of human beings and their societies depends upon the Church of Jesus Christ seeking to fulfill the Great Commission."[4] Now this may seem like a very limited view, until one recognizes that it is only through the ministry of radically devoted followers of Jesus that the kingdom of God comes in all its fullness.

At the heart of the commission to make disciples is the command to baptize. But before we get into the usual debates about infant and believer's baptism (how old one must be, or how much water should be used, and so on), let us start with the end in mind. Based on the Great Commission, we will focus on baptism as an initiation into the life of discipleship and a participation in the mission of God. Furthermore, we will see why this requires a dedication to the pursuit of holiness made possible only by collaboration in disciple-making fellowship.

When we lose sight of these ends, the practice of baptism can all too easily become an end in itself. Without teaching people how to grow as whole-life and lifelong disciples of Jesus, mission gets reduced to making converts, and the baptism of converts or cradle-Christians gets reduced to making church members. It is one thing to be baptized in the name of the Father, but quite another thing to hunger and thirst for the kingdom of God. It is one thing to be baptized in the name of the Son, but quite another thing to follow Jesus' way of life. It is one thing to be baptized in the name of the Spirit, but quite another thing to be filled with the Spirit's power for discipleship and mission. This book is about our vocation to live as mission-shaped disciples in disciple-making communities and how baptism lies at the heart of that calling.

THE BIRTH OF A DISCIPLESHIP MOVEMENT

We cannot understand the meaning of baptism apart from reflecting on the baptism of Jesus himself and all that followed in his own life. And we cannot understand the Great Commission apart from the way Jesus baptized his own disciples and trained them to share in his disciple-making ministry.

The Baptism of Jesus

Jesus commanded his apostles to make disciples by baptizing them in the name of the Father, the Son, and the Holy Spirit. This pattern recalls what happened at the baptism of Jesus. When he emerged from the water, the Spirit descended upon him in the form of a dove, and the Father bore witness that this was his Son, whom he loved (Mt 3:13-17). Clearly, Jesus did not need to be baptized as a means of purification from sin. Rather, his baptism is best seen as setting an example for his followers of what it means to be immersed in the mission of the triune God. For him, it was a commissioning into his Messianic ministry; and for us, it is a co-missioning as his disciples to share in his ministry of advancing the kingdom of God throughout the world.

After his baptism, Jesus was led by the Spirit into the wilderness to be tempted by the devil. All the temptations he faced were intended to question the identity he received in baptism and derail him from the mission of God. Instead, he overcame temptation in the power of the Spirit by remembering his identity as the faithful Son of God and the joy of sharing in the work of his Father. After returning to Galilee full of the Spirit, he entered the synagogue in his hometown of Nazareth and announced his mission to the world: "The Spirit of the Lord is upon me, because he has anointed me to proclaim good news," which was "the good news of the kingdom of God" brought near in word and deed (Lk 4:18, 43).

This captures perfectly the connection between baptism, discipleship, and mission. On the one hand, baptism propels us into a Spirit-filled life of discipleship, in which we overcome the power of sin, the flesh, and the devil. On the other hand, we are set free for a Spirit-anointed life of mission to become co-workers with Jesus in the kingdom. It is only by following in the way of Jesus that the good news is proclaimed to the poor, the hungry are fed, and the naked are clothed; that prisoners are set free, the sick are healed, and the brokenhearted are comforted; that sinners are forgiven, the dead are brought back to life, and the world is reconciled to God. This mission-shaped discipleship does not come naturally; it is not accomplished in a moment; it is going to be costly; and it must be intentionally developed.

The Baptism of the Disciples

One puzzling question about baptism in the Gospels is whether the first disciples were themselves baptized; and, if so, were they baptized by Jesus? The witness of Scripture is not clear. We know that John the Baptist came baptizing people as a sign of repentance and purification and that he baptized Jesus. In the Gospel of John, we are told that John the Baptist had been preparing a way for Jesus, who would forgive sins and baptize people in the Spirit. After hearing this message, at least two of his own disciples decided to follow Jesus (Jn 1:29-40).

Shortly after, Jesus told Nicodemus that no one could enter the kingdom unless they are born of water and the Spirit. We then find Jesus performing baptisms in the countryside, and his disciples were with him. In a further encounter with John the Baptist, Jesus is described as the one who "gives the Spirit without measure" (Jn 3:22-36). Just a little later, the Scripture implies that more and more people started coming to Jesus for baptism, although it was his disciples who were actually baptizing them (4:1-2).

Looking back at this record, we can make three tentative conclusions. First, it makes sense that Jesus would have baptized his own disciples, at least in the beginning, and most likely the twelve apostles. Second, it hardly seems likely that Jesus would authorize the apostles to baptize others if he had not baptized them himself. Third, it is equally unlikely that others would submit themselves for baptism by the apostles unless it was well known that Jesus himself had baptized them. Delegating the responsibility of baptizing his other followers to the apostles was part of their training in the art of making disciples. Jesus was already investing in them as missionaries or "sent ones" with authority to make disciples in his name.

From this perspective, the Great Commission was the natural continuation of a ministry Jesus had already begun to share with the first disciples. The resurrection of Jesus was also an affirmation of his mission and ministry, including his particular method of making disciples and training disciple makers. The Father said, "Yes" to the work of his Son by raising him from the dead and bestowing on him all authority in heaven and earth to finish what he started. "Therefore," Jesus said, "Go and make disciples of all nations." In other words, they were to continue what they had been doing all along, but now their mission would extend beyond Israel to the rest of the world.

The Disciple-Making Community

The mission of Jesus was to save the whole world. From the time of his baptism, which marked the beginning of his public ministry, he had only three years to ensure this mission would be completed. His gospel of salvation was that the kingdom of God was near and the only way to enter the kingdom was to become his disciple. However, the task of making disciples is slow. There would always be a limit to what Jesus could accomplish in his own lifetime and geographical sphere of influence. The only way his mission could be completed was by teaching his own disciples how to bring others into the kingdom and having them teach the newly baptized disciples to do the same. So, the mission strategy of Jesus was to start a disciple-making movement that would continue from generation to generation and spread from place to place until it reached the ends of the earth.

Trained well, very ordinary people could become such multiplying disciples. Jesus staked his mission on equipping a few rather unpromising individuals and sending them out as partners in his disciple-making ministry. When he finally issued the Great Commission, it came as no surprise. By "baptize," he meant continue to baptize others as you have been baptized. By "teach," he meant train others as you have been trained. When we examine the method that Jesus used to teach his disciples, it looks more like apprenticeship than scholarship and more like spiritual formation than formal education.[5]

First, Jesus attracted the crowds. They came to hear his preaching about the kingdom of God and to witness it breaking in through the signs and wonders he performed. Second, Jesus attracted a group of around seventy followers. They gathered at his feet to hear his teaching, which was often a commentary on the example of his own life. Third, Jesus chose a small group of twelve apostles. They shared close fellowship with him, so he could mentor them as co-workers in the kingdom. Fourth, Jesus invested in three close friends. He often took Peter, James, and John aside from the rest of the twelve to share in the most profound moments of his life and ministry. This sharing was also preparation for what lay ahead. He invited them to share in his true vocation by raising a little girl from the dead (Mk 5:35-43). He invited them to share in his relationship with the Father by taking them up the Mount of Transfiguration (Lk 9:28-36). And he invited them to share in the way of the cross by witnessing his suffering in the garden of Gethsemane (Mt 26:36-46). Through all this, he was training them to know the joy and count the cost of sharing in his mission.

Over time, Jesus spent less and less time with the crowds but more and more time with the twelve. This hardly sounds like a recipe for successful global mission. But like mustard seeds and leaven in the lump, the life of the kingdom would spread by disciples who had tasted the power of the world to come and were committed to inviting others to the heavenly banquet. The strategy of Jesus was to impart the life of the kingdom to them by sharing his life with them. Through such mentoring, Jesus raised up disciples who shared his heart and imitated his life and taught others to do the same. Jesus was an imitator of the Father.[6] The disciples came to the Father by imitating Jesus, and the world would come to Jesus by imitating the disciples. No doubt, the admonition of Paul was one shared by all the apostles and those whom they trained as disciple makers: "Follow my example, as I follow the example of Christ" (1 Cor 11:1, also 4:16). In this way, the gospel and life of the kingdom was imparted, heart to heart, life to life, and nation to nation, to the end of the earth.

When the church baptizes people into the name of Jesus, it makes a commitment to train them in the way and mission of Jesus. It must do this by also adopting the method of Jesus. Disciples are best made in small learning communities, where people can be taught how to live as citizens of the kingdom and co-workers in mission. We certainly see this pattern in the origin and spread of the early Methodist movement, which began with a small group of hungry disciples in Oxford and grew into a worldwide connection of disciple-making communities.[7] Those communities also resembled the relational method of Jesus by gathering people into "classes" of about twelve people and even smaller groups called "bands" with the goal of conforming their whole lives to the likeness of Jesus from the inside out. What we may learn is that the Great Commission is not merely to pass on the gospel of the kingdom by any available means, but to pass on the very life of the kingdom by the methods that Jesus used.

THE METHOD OF MULTIPLYING DISCIPLES

The meaning of baptism cannot be abstracted from the mandate to go and make disciples. As we have already seen, the Great Commission was to be accomplished by teaching people, not merely baptizing them. For Jesus, teaching was not simply a matter of *informing* people about the *message* of the kingdom, but *imparting* to people the *life* of the kingdom. Let us take a closer look at the commission itself so we can draw out some of these connections.[8]

The King and His Commission

First, it is significant that Jesus agreed to rendezvous with the disciples up a mountain. We do not know where that was, but the "mountain" in Scripture was a place where heaven and earth met and a symbol for the presence of God. For that reason, it was the place of coronation for kings who would be the representatives of God's will on earth. So, when the disciples saw Jesus, they fell to their knees in worship. God had raised Jesus from the dead, affirming his mission and confirming him as King of the kingdom. The worship of the disciples was not merely an act of pious devotion.

It was a pledge of allegiance to their King and a recommitment to the life of discipleship. For those who had recently denied and betrayed him, this was a sign of their willingness to lay down their lives for him. Some, however, were of two minds.

Second, as King of the kingdom, Jesus claimed the authority of God to send his disciples out to continue his mission. This moment recalls the previous occasion when Jesus authorized them to proclaim the kingdom and demonstrate its proximity by healing the sick, raising the dead, and casting out evil spirits (Mt 10:5-8). At that time, they were sent out to the lost sheep of Israel, but now their mandate is extended to all the peoples of the world. Moreover, their mission was not merely to bring the kingdom near but to make new followers of the King. Jesus made them his disciples, and now they were being sent to make disciples of Jesus. As Mortimer Arias has succinctly put it, "mission is discipleship."[9] Or to put it another way, to be a disciple is to be a missionary. Disciples are not just "called" by Jesus, but are also "sent" by him as missionaries to the least and the lost.

Third, the commission to make disciples has the three key ingredients of going, baptizing, and teaching. They were to go and proclaim the gospel, inviting people to repent from their old ways in the world and commit to a new life in the kingdom. They were to baptize those who responded in faith as a sign of forgiveness, entering the kingdom, and pledging allegiance to the King. And they were to teach them how to give their lives to Jesus by living as citizens of his kingdom through obedience to his commands.

This way of discipleship can also be summed up in the words of the Great Commandment: "to love God with all our heart and to love our neighbor as ourselves" (Mt 22:36-40). In other words, we love God by a total submission to his reign, and we love our neighbor in the way that Jesus has loved us, by laying down our lives to bring them into his kingdom.

Finally, Jesus made a promise to the disciples that he would be with them always. The authority they had for mission was nothing other than the presence of the King in their midst. They were not sent out to make disciples *for* Jesus, but to make disciples *with* him, as co-workers in the kingdom. Being a disciple is not so much about obeying commands as following a person. Equally, making disciples is not about demanding obedience to rules but inviting others into a personal relationship with the One who changes lives. The motivation for mission is always a desire to introduce people to our risen King and the beauty of his kingdom.

It should be remembered that Jesus gave the Great Commission to all the disciples, including those who were filled with doubt. This serves as an encouragement to all who come after that sharing in the commission is not merely for the zealous, but for everyone who bows the knee to Jesus, even with fear and trembling. It also reminds us that the mission of making disciples always belongs to Jesus, and we depend entirely on his authority and power in our midst. The commands of Jesus cannot be fulfilled without the promised gift of the Spirit, who continues to make him present among us, reminds us of his teaching, and empowers our obedience (Jn 14:15-31).

Go, Baptize and Teach

Laying out the Great Commission this way helps us understand that the three commands to go, baptize, and teach are not separate activities, but each contributes to the single activity of making disciples. From this perspective, we can further define the practice of baptism in terms of the following four commitments.

First, baptism is a commitment to evangelistic mission. Baptism does not make sense apart from the practice of evangelism, conversion to Jesus, initiation into the kingdom of God, and the life of discipleship.[10] But it can also be observed that Jesus used the word "Go" in a present continuous tense that could be translated, "As you are going." From this perspective, it does not mean going overseas on long- or short-term mission projects. Nor does it mean staying to do the same kind of projects with needy people at home. Rather, it implies that the business of making disciples is something that emerges organically as we go through everyday life and among the networks of relationships we make along the way. This is what Jesus did, and it has implications for all of us. Wherever we might live, the mission field is on the doorstep of our everyday lives. For some of us, going where Jesus sends will mean leaving home and living with a doorstep that opens onto a very unfamiliar world. But for all of us, going where Jesus sends means crossing the threshold as ordinary missionaries into a world that needs to hear the gospel.

Second, baptism is a commitment to practical mentoring. Jesus said, "Teach them to obey everything I have commanded you." On the one hand, doing this "as we go" means that our teaching will be rooted in the witness and example of our daily lives. On the other hand, the emphasis is on the word "obey" rather than "everything." In other words, the real challenge is not merely helping new disciples to understand all the commands of Jesus, but helping them to put his teaching into practice.[11] The perennial challenge facing discipleship is not knowing what we should do; it is doing what we already know we should do. In other words, the challenge is obedience. Equally, discipleship training is not about slavish legalism to an impossible standard of values and rules. It is about a way of life that is marked by joyful obedience, flowing from the heart of our new identity as children of God.

Third, baptism is a commitment to be a disciple-making community. We must remember that Jesus is not addressing a collection of individual leaders but a community of disciples. He is inviting them to fulfill his commission as co-workers with him. Again, his promise to be with them is not an assurance that he will remain with each one individually but that he will abide among them all as a community. It takes a community of discipleship, gathered around the feet of Jesus, to teach others his way of life. As people on the go, we should be imparting the message and life of the kingdom by starting disciple-making communities wherever we are and wherever our travels may take us.

Fourth, baptism is a commitment to raising ordinary missionaries. It is not possible to enter the kingdom of God as a follower of Jesus and not become a participant in his mission. For one thing, all the teaching of Jesus is about what it means to participate in the kingdom, as both citizen and servant. For another thing, being obedient to the Great Commission is itself part of the "everything" we are meant to teach others, from generation to generation.

Disciples Who Make Disciples

From first to the last, these four commitments are circular. The commission is to go and make disciples, who will join us in the commission to go and make disciples. In other words, discipleship should be missional and reproductive by nature. Indeed, we should be concerned about any Christian community that exhibits a long-term failure to make new disciples. It should be seen as a symptom of spiritual sterility that demands a re-examination of its baptismal practice. In the coming chapters, we will see how the fruitfulness of early Methodism as a disciple-making movement embodied these commitments and indirectly challenged the baptismal integrity of the Church of England in its own day.

THE MISSIONARY NATURE OF BAPTISM

The book of Acts shows us how the Great Commission was worked out in practice by the apostles. The risen Jesus told the disciples, "You will receive power when the Holy Spirit comes on you; and you will be my witnesses in Jerusalem, and in all Judea and Samaria, and to the ends of the earth" (Acts 1:8). After Pentecost, the preaching of Peter led to the birth of the church in Jerusalem (2:42-47). As a result, "the word of God spread" and "the number of disciples in Jerusalem increased rapidly" (6:7). Then, after the martyrdom of Stephen and the conversion of Paul, the gospel spread through "all Judea, Galilee, and Samaria." The church "was strengthened," such that "living in the fear of the Lord and encouraged by the Holy Spirit, it increased in numbers" (9:31). Peter then took the gospel from the coast to Syria and, despite persecution, "the word of God continued to spread and flourish" (12:24). Paul began his missionary journey by going to Cyprus and Galatia, and "the churches were strengthened in the faith and grew daily in numbers" (16:5). Then he traveled from Syria to Macedonia, Achaia, Asia, and back again to Ephesus. "In this way the word of the Lord spread widely and grew in power" (19:20). Finally, after revisiting Macedonia and Achaia, Paul ended up in Rome where "he proclaimed the kingdom of God and taught about the Lord Jesus Christ—with all boldness and without hindrance" (28:31).

It is worth noting that when the Scripture speaks about "the word" growing and spreading from place to place, it does not imply the mass communication of a disembodied message. Nor does it refer simply to the ministry of the apostles themselves. Like Jesus before them, the apostles brought the kingdom near in word and deed. Hearing the gospel with faith meant adopting a whole new way of life by following the example of the apostles, and this included the responsibility to pass on the message in the same way they had received it (Acts 20:13-38; 2 Thes 3:9; Heb 13:7).

When the Scripture speaks of numerical growth, it should not conjure up images of great congregations and megachurches. Rather, this way of life was expressed and passed on by the multiplication of relatively small house fellowships. These communities functioned as extended families who reached out to incorporate friends, neighbors, strangers, and even adversaries into their midst. Apostles and evangelists led people out to proclaim the gospel of new life in Christ, while pastors and teachers stayed home to nurture the disciple-making community.[12] Outsiders were incorporated into these new households of faith through baptism and joined their collective mission in the world.

New Life in Disciple-Making Community

We get an insight into how baptism was understood through the letters written to the little house churches in this expanding movement. They provide us with a range of images, which is one reason we have differences of theology and practice in later church traditions. Putting those differences aside for the time being, there is wide agreement on two broad themes.

First, baptism is "the sign of new life through Jesus Christ."[13] As such, it has been thought of as dying and rising with Christ (Rom 6:3-5; Col 2:12), putting off our old life in the world and putting on the new life in Christ (Gal 3:27), passing from darkness into the light of Christ (Eph 5:14), washing away of sin and being set apart for holy living under the Lordship of Christ (1 Cor 6:11). We enter this new life through water and the Spirit, like being born anew into the family of God (Jn 3:5-7), or washed and renewed for a life of faithful obedience (Tit 3:3-8). Baptism is not just a sign of new life in its beginning, but an ongoing commitment to active discipleship that flows from it.

Second, baptism is "a sign and seal of our common discipleship."[14] It is a mark of unity with Christians everywhere, signified through incorporation into the fellowship of a local church. The symbolism of water is connected to the story of God's saving acts in the Old Testament that helped to shape Israel as his own people. In the days of Noah, God provided an ark to save eight people from a corrupt world through the waters of the flood. So now, through the death and resurrection of Jesus, all people can be saved from the powers of this world through the waters of baptism (1 Pet 3:18-22). In the days of Moses, God rescued his people from slavery in Egypt by enabling them to pass through the sea and provided them with spiritual food and drink in the wilderness. So now, we make an exodus from the sinful ways of this world by passing through the waters of baptism and feeding on the body and blood of Christ (1 Cor 10:1-4, 14-17).

Through baptism, we enter new life in Christ by joining the people of God and participating in his great plan of salvation for the world. We who were once outside the covenant of promise have been drawn in to form a new community in which the ancient barriers of gender, race, and social status are overcome (Eph 2:15; Gal 3:27-28; 1 Cor 12:13). Baptism is not just a sign of belonging, but of reaching out to draw others into this new life in Christ, through the fellowship of his disciple-making community.

The Moment and the Movement

We are going to look more closely at how the practice of baptism weaves together these familiar themes of new life and fellowship and how it has varied from one tradition to another. For now, however, it is sufficient to note these images do not arise from the static context of denominational structures but from the more dynamic context of a disciple-making movement. If we remember only the moment of baptism, we all too easily end up with cheap grace by settling for the assurance of conversion, or by holding onto our identity as children of God while failing to walk worthy of it. If we remember baptism as a moment that immerses us in a movement, however, we will find Jesus calling us into deeper discipleship and sending us out to share his mission in the world.

There is one sense in which baptism signifies a converting moment when we make a decision to turn our backs on the old life and put it to death. But there is another sense in which baptism is embarking on a journey of discipleship that requires us to deny ourselves and take up our cross daily as lifelong and whole-life followers of Jesus (Mt 16:24). It is one thing to be forgiven, washed clean, and receive the light of Christ; and yet another thing to pursue holy lives that shine like stars in a dark world, through the life-transforming power of the Spirit within (Phil 2:15-16).

Or again, there is one sense in which baptism signifies our welcome into the community of disciples as members of the church. But there is another sense in which baptism leads to our participation in the body of Christ as those variously gifted by his Spirit for ministry and mission (Eph 4:3-13). It is one thing for us to join the people of God and yet another thing for the people of God to join his mission in the world. Baptism in the early church was certainly not an end in itself but the moment of immersion into a disciple-making movement that sweeps us up into God's life-giving mission to all nations.

As we go through this book, we will see how Wesley and the early Methodists embodied this movement of discipleship and work backward to see how it connects to the moment of baptism. One of the key questions for Wesleyan communities today is whether a denominational church can recover the characteristics of such a disciple-making movement.

MISSION-SHAPED BAPTISM IN PRACTICE

We will conclude this chapter with two stories about how I have seen the threads of baptism, discipleship, and mission woven together in contemporary church practice. The first is an example of believer's baptism, and the second is the baptism of an infant.

Tom Hardwick became a member of our church in Chesterfield (UK) after a wonderful conversion to Christ through participation in an evangelistic program called the Alpha Course.[15] In fact, his whole family made commitments to Christ and presented themselves for baptism. Tom inherited Duchenne Muscular Dystrophy and began developing the symptoms of the condition when he was five years old. His movement is severely limited, and he is largely confined to a wheelchair. At the service of baptism, he gave a very meaningful testimony to the healing and life-transforming power of the new life he had received in Christ. When it came to being baptized, Tom's body was placed in a sling and suspended over the pool water. After the elders had climbed into the pool, Tom was slowly lowered and fully immersed in the water, then raised up again to face the future as a baptized follower of Jesus. From that moment, he grew in spirit, went to Bible college, and is developing an itinerant preaching ministry to inspire hope and release faith in others. Tom has a serious muscle-wasting disease, but his life is "not wasted."[16] Baptism for Tom was an initiation into the life of discipleship and a participation in the mission of God.

A few years ago, I was at a conference in Oxford. One Sunday morning, I decided to visit a local evangelical Anglican church. As part of the service, a young couple in the church brought their baby to be baptized. For the most part, the service was very familiar, as the vicar invited parents and godparents to make vows that they would raise the child as a disciple of Jesus. As I expected, he also invited the church to welcome the child into their fellowship and commit to supporting the parents in their vocation. What did take me by surprise, however, was a penetrating question to the parents, testing the seriousness of their disciple-making commitment. I am recalling this from memory, so it won't be verbatim, but you will get the gist of the question: "Will you raise this child to be a faithful follower of Jesus and support him in his discipleship, even if the path he chooses might lead to suffering or death?" I expect they had been prepared for this question. They gave their whole-hearted affirmation, and the boy was baptized. This was most definitely about initiating the baby into a life of discipleship by a community of disciples participating in the mission of God.

REMEMBERING OUR BAPTISM

At the beginning of this chapter, I said we would be addressing the question: "What has baptism got to do with mission?" Focusing on the Great Commission, I have argued that the answer is, "Discipleship." Not just any discipleship, but mission-shaped discipleship in a disciple-making community. From this perspective, I suggest we can think of baptism as having four interrelated characteristics that beg four underlying questions:

- **Initiation into the life of discipleship**. Baptism is not just a mark of conversion or church membership. It is about becoming a lifelong and whole-life follower of Jesus. The question is, "How do we work out our discipleship in daily living?"
- **Dedication to the pursuit of holiness**. To grow as a disciple means becoming more like Jesus in heart and life, in word and deed, at church and in daily life. The question is, "How does holy living make us witnesses to the kingdom of God?"
- **Participation in the mission of God**. Growing in the likeness of Jesus also means sharing in his ministry as a citizen and servant of the kingdom, including the mandate to spread the gospel and make new disciples. The question is, "How do we share our life of discipleship as everyday missionaries?"
- **Collaboration in disciple-making fellowship**. The vocation of growing as a disciple and fulfilling the commission to make disciples cannot be done on our own. Presenting a credible witness to the kingdom and helping one another thrive under the reign of God takes a whole community

of disciples and co-workers in the gospel. The question is, "How do we help one another live as mission-shaped followers of Jesus?"

Each of the following chapters will conclude by thinking about these four marks as a way of remembering our baptism. In the next chapter, we explore more fully how baptism makes us all participants in the Great Commission and what it means for our discipleship to become missional by nature.

QUESTIONS FOR GROUP DISCUSSION

1. After reading this chapter, how have your views changed about baptism and discipleship?
2. Why does it take fully committed followers of Jesus to make authentic new disciples?
3. What has the Great Commandment got to do with the Great Commission? How is the love of God connected to the love of neighbor? And how is love of neighbor expressed in helping neighbors become disciples?
4. In what ways do the two examples of mission-shaped baptism challenge you to think about the connection between baptism, discipleship, and mission? How does this cause you to reflect on your church's practice of baptism?
5. Which parts of the fourfold pattern for remembering our baptism at the conclusion of this chapter do you find the most challenging? How is the Spirit guiding you?

CHAPTER 2

The Cost of Remembrance

Remember your baptism and be thankful . . . The Holy Spirit work within you, that having been born through water and the Spirit, you may live as a faithful disciple of Jesus Christ.[1]

Remembering our baptism means the decision to deny ourselves and follow Jesus must be made on a daily basis. Are you counting the cost of living as a disciple who is on mission with God in the midst of everyday life?

Liturgies of baptism may invite those who are already baptized to reaffirm their faith by remembering their own baptism. This is meant to inspire thankfulness, not merely for the occasion of our baptism but for the ongoing work of the Spirit in our hearts that empowers us to grow as faithful disciples in daily life. But we have seen that remembering our baptism can easily become a means of cheap grace. In our self-centeredness, we like to remember what God's love has done *for* us, but forget what this love requires *from* us, both as individuals and the church. In this chapter, we will face what it means to count the cost of being disciples who live as those who are "sent" into the world as everyday missionaries.

When I say remembering "our" baptism, I don't just mean reflecting on what it means for us to live as baptized individuals, but reflecting on the nature of baptism as a missionary practice in the church. If we are to become authentic disciple-making communities, we must count the cost of discipleship, not merely as individuals but also in our life together as the church. The secret to counting the cost of discipleship and mission is being motivated by the love of God and neighbor. It demands that we lay down our lives for the sake of the kingdom and invite others to do the same. John Stott argued that there is no Great Commission without the Great Commandment.[2] Remembering our baptism will mean counting the cost of a life worthy of the love we have received, "for Christ's love compels us" (2 Cor 5:14). To do this, we will start by looking back at the history of the Great Commission for insight into the present state of the church and to gain some wisdom for the future.

Remembering the Great Commission

From the Reformation onward, the Great Commission has shaped the broad tradition of evangelicalism and has been a major source of inspiration for the development of modern missions.[3] So, we will begin to remember our baptism by reflecting on how the Puritan, Pietist, and Revivalist streams of evangelical spirituality have given shape to the missionary movement and their influence on the missional impulses of early Methodism.

The Cost of Discipleship and Mission

With the migration of Puritans to America, the conversion of native Indians became an expression of their missionary spirit, albeit intermixed with colonial ambition. This mission was never systematically extended but did produce outstanding figures like

David Brainerd (1718–1747), who gave his short life to working among the Delaware Indians of New Jersey. John Wesley published an extract of Brainerd's journal as an example for his preachers.[4] He said, "Let us be followers of him, as he was of Christ, in absolute self-devotion, in total deadness to the world, and in fervent love to God and man."[5] Brainerd set a pattern of missionary zeal, motivated by a genuine love for the lost. Wesley commended his example of costly discipleship, simplicity of life, and sheer generosity with the little he had. In addition, he noted how the fruitfulness of Brainerd's work could not be separated from a dedication to fasting and prayer. He was presented as a model of how perseverance through terrible bouts of sickness and depression could lead to spiritual growth and effective ministry. Wesley's account of his life became recommended reading for many ordinary members of the Methodist societies.

The Community of Discipleship and Mission

The missionary movement was really pioneered by the Continental Pietists, especially the Moravians, with their emphasis on the need for personal conversion and holy living.[6] In 1727, under the leadership of Count Zinzendorf, the Moravian settlement at Herrnhut experienced a season of community renewal. Their hearts were set on fire with love for God, for one another, and for spreading the gospel abroad. They nurtured the new life of discipleship through fellowship bands and other small groups, dedicated to praying for their own discipleship and witness. From these small beginnings, a community of about three hundred members with meager resources became the epicenter for mission work around the world. Over a period of thirty years or so, hundreds of Moravian missionaries were sent out in twos and threes to renew the churches of Europe by calling nominal Christians to serious discipleship. They introduced people to the gospel by gathering them into small groups for prayer, Bible study, and spiritual guidance. Over time, this method was extended to the Inuit of Greenland, slaves in the West Indies, American Indians in Pennsylvania, and beyond. These missionaries were not theologically trained or financially supported clergy, but zealous laypeople who were often given just enough money to get to the nearest port. They took up ordinary work to support their mission in some of the most remote and challenging parts of the world. Of course, Moravian missionaries were instrumental in the "conversion" of John Wesley to evangelical Christianity, and so helped to shape the very origins of the early Methodist movement.

The Power for Discipleship and Mission

For much of the eighteenth century, England and America were caught up in a long season of revival, also known as the "Great Awakening." In times of revival, the Spirit awakens the church to its own lukewarm faith, the need for conversion, and the promises of saving grace. Alongside this, the Spirit also implants a hunger for deeper relationship with God, a renewed passion for the life of discipleship, and a zeal for evangelistic mission. Leaders of the Great Awakening like Jonathan Edwards (1703–1758) helped shape a theology of revival. He described the fruit of true conversion as a deep joy that overflows in a desire for holy living and a zeal for spreading the gospel. The marks of true revival are a deeper devotion to Jesus, freedom from the power of sin, commitment to scriptural Christianity, a conscience guided by the Spirit of truth, and the pursuit of holy love for God and neighbor. In short, revival points to the work of the Spirit, transforming us into the likeness of Jesus and empowering us to share in his mission. Wesley's theology of conversion and discipleship was profoundly influenced by this revival spirituality, and he published several edited versions of Edwards's writings for the people called Methodists.[7]

The Ecumenical Impulse of Discipleship and Mission

From these accounts, we see how the missionary movement was promoted by a willingness to count the cost of discipleship, supported by disciple-making community, and motivated by a zealous love for God and neighbor. As far as I can see, however, there is little evidence that this movement promoted much sustained theological reflection on the missional significance of baptism. On the one hand, church leaders and missionaries operated within the context of their own received traditions. This was certainly true for Wesley, as we shall see. On the other hand, the missionary movement had an ecumenical impulse that viewed historic contentions about churchmanship as secondary to the task of saving souls. This can also be seen in Wesley's sermon, "The Catholic Spirit." He said, "I ask not, Are you of my Church" or what you do "in the administration of baptism."[8] Rather, he urged Christians of all backgrounds simply to love and uphold one another in prayer and strengthen one another's hands in the work of God.

THE WHOLE SPIRIT OF MISSIONARIES

Wesley expected his leaders in the early Methodist movement to embody the Great Commission, according to the scriptural pattern we discussed in chapter one. This is clearly seen in his instructions to the Methodist preachers who were to set an example for the movement as a whole.

The Priority of Evangelistic Mission

Wesley told his preachers, "You have nothing to do but to save souls." Therefore, "go always, not only to those who want you, but to those who want you most."[9] His preachers were always on the move from person to person, house to house, town to town, and even nation to nation. Preaching the gospel was not merely a strategy; it was a way of life. For Wesley, the business of saving souls was about making disciples, not just converts. It was simply not enough to set forth Christ as justifying us with his blood without opening hearts to the sanctifying work of his Spirit. In other words, Wesley insisted they must proclaim the whole gospel by making perfection in love the goal of evangelism and discipleship. "Destroy this hope, and salvation stands still, or rather decreases daily."[10]

The Need for Practical Mentoring

Wesley expected the preachers to "go into every house in course, and teach everyone therein, young and old . . . to be Christians, inwardly and outwardly."[11] He was clear that preaching by itself would not make disciples, so he instructed them to go and teach people face-to-face. Unless they met with their hearers to converse about their daily walk with God, any good done through preaching would quickly die away. Visitation was to be done, whether a leader felt gifted for it or not, and whether the people desired to receive it or not: "Gift or no gift, you are to do this, or else you are not called to be a Methodist preacher."[12] This ministry was crucial to the task of evangelism, growth in grace, and fanning the flame of spiritual zeal. Wesley was convinced that without such mentoring, the whole movement would die.

The Methods of Disciple-Making Community

Wesley made it clear there was no such thing as a "solitary Christian." It is not possible to seek faith, or pursue the life of discipleship, or engage in mission on our own. He was keenly aware of the constant threat of straying from the way of Jesus and the subtle temptation to justify our waywardness. Wesley learned from the Moravians that the only cure was "watching over one another in love." The responsibility for teaching one another to obey the commands of Jesus in early Methodism was largely fulfilled through the practice of small-group fellowship. Class meetings of around twelve people were organized for seekers and believers to hold one another accountable for their discipleship and especially for using the spiritual disciplines as means of grace. Band meetings of around five people were organized for believers pressing on to perfection, so they could share life deeply as fellow travelers and spiritual guides. The class meeting was the basic unit of membership in a Methodist society. So, at some level, everyone contributed to the task of disciple making. We shall explore this more fully later.

The Importance of Raising Missionaries

One question the preachers asked in conference was this: "Why are we not more wholly devoted to God, breathing the whole spirit of missionaries"? Or, to put it another way: "Why is the Methodist movement not advancing as it should?" Their answer is rather shocking: "Because we are idle!" So they were urged to remember the life of David Brainerd, who spent his life in the work of God.

Making disciples is hard work, and finding ways to avoid it or creating substitutes for it is a constant temptation for those in leadership. The issue is not really how much work we are doing but what kind of work will be effective in making disciples and raising missionaries. In the first place, Wesley constantly reinforced the need for his preachers to work out their own salvation with fear and trembling. Only then would they have a heart for co-working with God in the salvation of others as living examples and mentors on the journey of discipleship.

There are no substitutes for this costly form of disciple making, as much as we would prefer to find programs that will do the work for us. Of course, running programs in the church can be hard work, and some people may find them to be a means of grace. But they do not make great demands on our discipleship as leaders. Following in the footsteps of Jesus and Wesley will mean counting the cost of nurturing our own spiritual life and the deeply personal cost of sharing that life with others.

Wesley knew that the challenge for new converts was the temptation to settle for "a sort of confidence that God will save them, while the world has their hearts."[13] Making disciples was about dispelling this misunderstanding and enabling people to live for the glory of God. He said, if this "common ignorance were banished, and the people in every house and every shop were busied in speaking the word and works of God, surely the Lord would dwell in our habitations." The natural consequence of authentic spiritual leadership among the preachers would be the formation of ordinary disciples as everyday missionaries.

THE GREAT COMMISSION FOR EVERYONE

These days, it has become rather commonplace for us to hear the Great Commission as a word that addresses everyone in the church. But it has not always been this way. In the eighteenth century, many interpreted it as a command given specifically to the first apostles and that the book of Acts tells us how it was finished. This view tended to receive support from those of a more Calvinist persuasion, who argued that God would bring about the salvation of the world in his own time and didn't really need human help to accomplish it. William Carey (1761–1834) was a Baptist pastor steeped in the Calvinist tradition who challenged these widely held views. Drawing on the latest ethnographical data, Carey showed that the Great Commission was far from completed and that it was the responsibility of the whole church to join in advancing this missionary task.[14]

The Formation of Mission Societies

Carey urged those with a heart for mission to gather in societies and pray for the work of God. They would also raise money to "support the ministry of the gospel at home, and to encourage *village preaching* in our respective neighbourhoods." Any surplus would be used "to defray the expenses of carrying the gospel into the heathen world."[15] This led to the formation of the Baptist Missionary Society and set a pattern for the development of missionary societies across the denominations. It is interesting to note that Carey's vision was for mission that started at home and then spread overseas, like the pattern set out in the Book of Acts, where the gospel witness would move from Jerusalem to the ends of the earth.

Carey's work promoted a tradition of praying for mission partners overseas and collecting money to support their sending agencies. I suggest, however, this strategy for world mission carried the seeds of its own ultimate failure at home. It is one thing to involve everyone as supporters of mission, but another thing for everyone to be active participants in the Great Commission. Carey succeeded in overturning the idea that God alone was responsible for the conversion of the world by exchanging it for the belief that God calls a relatively few special people to fulfill his mission. For the vast majority of ordinary disciples, their part in the commission was simply reduced to prayer and financing the work of others.

The Church as a Mission Society

Carey's strategy might have seemed unproblematic through the long era of Christendom, when the surrounding culture at home was at least nominally Christian. While those with missionary zeal were sent overseas, the culture at home began its slide toward post-Christendom. The denominational churches in the West have been declining in number and vitality ever since. Today, our home nations have become a mission field in their own right, and we welcome missionaries back from our daughter churches to re-evangelize their spiritual parents.

Over the last thirty years or so, there has been a growing recognition of the need to adopt a more missionary stance toward the spread of the gospel at home.[16] In some ways, Carey's vision for the mission society has been re-imagined as a vision for the church itself. There is growing consensus that churches become more missional when they live intentionally as communities of discipleship, which gather together in order to send one another out as everyday missionaries.[17] When Jesus sends us out to "all nations," that includes our own. The first disciples began their mission at home, among the Jews. That work was extended into all the world, not abandoned at home (Acts 1:8). When Jesus said he would be with them "to the very end of the age," we now understand that it would take multiple generations of multiplying disciples for the Great Commission to be fulfilled.

THE GREAT OMISSION FROM THE GREAT COMMISSION

Remembering our baptism should counter our forgetfulness that the Great Commission is for everyone by reminding us that all Christians are called to live as everyday missionaries. But many churches are a long way from being mission societies, and our members are a long way from living as mission-shaped disciples.

The Challenge to Evangelize

During his inaugural address as President of the British Methodist Conference in 2015, the Rev. Steven Wild urged the denomination to "take God seriously" in the task of evangelism.[18] He urged them "to put mission on the agenda and give our churches an aim to win a person for Christ" and repeated the challenge "to bring one person to faith—to make one new member." It's telling that he had to remind them, "It's not impossible!" As a commission for the year ahead, he said, "Let's make bringing people to faith the main point, we don't do it alone. The unconditional love of Jesus is our motivation."

Wild led the way by example. He spent the year traveling around the United Kingdom by public transport with the intention of meeting ordinary people and sharing the love of Jesus with them. Throughout the year, his social media presence lit up with one story after another of people being "led to Christ" and taking steps of faith. From what I can tell, many ordinary disciples in the churches were inspired, though some doubted! What I cannot tell is how many of those were moved to follow his example, or whether his challenge was ultimately successful.

Wild also drew the Methodist Church's attention to its Deed of Union, which states, "It ever remembers that in the providence of God, Methodism was raised up to spread scriptural holiness through the land by the proclamation of the evangelical faith and declares its unfaltering resolve to be true to its divinely appointed mission."[19] This calls for the church "to have confidence in the full glory of Christian discipleship." But Wild's challenge also raises some troubling questions: Why has the church forgotten that evangelism and mission is its very reason for being? Why should it have to be reminded to "take God seriously" and that it's not impossible for us to fulfill this vocation? And why is the aim of bringing just one person to faith in a year such a serious challenge in the first place?

The Failure of Evangelism

Thinking about evangelistic mission as leading people to Christ and making converts has become highly ambiguous these days.

We have begun to notice that there is a wide difference between making converts and making disciples who will actually lay down their lives for Jesus and his kingdom. At its best, the strategy of making converts will also aim at incorporation into a local church where they might be taught how to follow Jesus as whole-life and lifelong disciples. The problem is, our local churches have not been in the business of making and nurturing this kind of discipleship. Instead, the glory of discipleship has been reduced to the benefits and responsibilities of church membership. Once we have settled for making members, however, we not only lose sight of making disciples, but the evangelical impulse to make converts gets lost as well.

The problem is circular. When there is little expectation that church members will grow in grace themselves, there will be little expectation of witness in their daily lives. The church enters a spiral of decline that quenches the whole spirit of missionaries outlined above. We are not raising missionaries, because we are not disciple-making communities. We are not disciple-making communities, because we are not mentoring people in the way of Jesus. And we are not mentoring people in the way of Jesus, because we are not committed to evangelistic mission. Perhaps remembering our baptism will mean that the church itself needs to be re-evangelized.

The Hope for Evangelistic Mission

As timely and appropriate as Wild's call to evangelism may be, it is doomed to failure unless churches are committed to making disciples. When Jesus first sent out his twelve disciples, he summed up their commission with the words, "Freely you have received, now freely give" (Mt 10:8). Jesus shared with them the new life of the kingdom, now they were to share it with others. So, the heart of the problem is that we cannot share what we do not have! This is what Dallas Willard refers to as the "Great Disparity" between "the hope for life expressed in Jesus" and "the actual day-to-day behavior, inner life, and social presence of most of those who now profess adherence to him."[20] This disparity exists because of our failure to make disciples. It is the "Great Omission" from our Great Commission.

The Great Omission leads to the idea that we can be good churchgoing Christians without being committed whole-life disciples. When we settle for this, our aim is often to make more members in order to stem numerical decline. We then assume our greatest need is better education, greater resources, or more effective projects and programs. But Jesus had none of these. Rather, Willard argues that "all it needs to fulfill Christ's purposes on earth is the quality of life he makes real in the life of his disciples."[21] It is this quality of life that we will be exploring throughout this book. For now, however, let me briefly observe a great omission in the account of both Wild and Willard. Neither of them pays attention to the connection between baptism, discipleship, and mission. What if the church had a better theology and practice of baptism that reconnects the need for both conversion and discipleship?

THE NEED FOR MISSION-SHAPED DISCIPLES

Wesley believed the Spirit is at work throughout the world in the heart of every human being, preparing each person to hear the gospel. He called this "prevenient grace." The same God who sends us out to share the gospel is already at work among those to whom we are sent, so they might respond with faith. But this truth begs a question: "If the gospel is truly good news and the Spirit is drawing all people to Jesus, why is it that so many people resist and reject our witness?"

God's Mission

Nearly a decade before Carey's treatise on the Great Commission, Wesley addressed the question of world mission in his sermon, "The General Spread of the Gospel."[22] He outlined the same kind of ethnographic data about unreached people that had an impact on Carey, but provided a much deeper theological account of what it actually means to participate in the mission of God.

Wesley's reflections emerged from the context of revival and the role of the early Methodist movement in God's ultimate purposes for world mission. He claimed, "We have strong reason to hope that the work he hath begun, he will carry on unto the day of the Lord Jesus; that he will never intermit this blessed work of his Spirit until he has fulfilled all his promises, until he hath put a period to sin, and misery, and infirmity, and death; and re-established universal holiness and happiness, and caused all the inhabitants of the earth to sing together, Hallelujah! The Lord God Omnipotent reigneth!"[23] God has a mission, and one day he will finish what he started.

God's Method of Mission

Although God could work irresistibly to convert the whole world, as the Calvinists might imagine,[24] Wesley argued that the "general manner of God's working" is rather more gradual and cooperative. "In general, it seems, the kingdom of God . . . will silently increase, wherever it is set up, and spread from heart to heart, from house to house, from town to town, from one kingdom to another."[25] If Wesley is right, participation in the mission of God is ultimately a question of discipleship.

So, what gets in the way of people hearing and responding to the gospel? Wesley's answer is startlingly simple, yet profoundly challenging for all its simplicity. The "grand stumbling-block" to the general spread of the gospel is "the lives of Christians." In other words, baptized members of the church. It is not difficult to sense his concerns about nominalism, formalism, legalism, hypocrisy, worldliness, and division. But Wesley was more concerned about what was lacking from their inward life that gave rise to all these outward problems. In other words, was the kingdom of God in their hearts so that they were known for "righteousness, peace, and joy in the Holy Spirit" (Rom 14:17)? Were they growing in the likeness of Jesus and walking as he walked? Wesley was bold enough to answer, "Nay, they are as far from it as hell is from heaven!"[26]

The kingdom of God is brought near in lives that are transformed by the Spirit from the inside out. The gospel is not only a message to be proclaimed but a reality to be encountered in people who are filled, transformed, and overflowing with the holy love of God and neighbor. Evangelism is not merely about sharing a faith we have believed but sharing the life we have received. This "silent" increase is not an appeal to evangelism without words, as though the gospel can spread without being heard. Rather, Wesley was saying that an endless series of noisy and spectacular revival meetings will not win the world. It takes the everyday relationships of people whose lives have been transformed by the truths they profess.

God's Everyday Missionaries

When the lives of Christians are really transformed by the gospel, Wesley believed that others might "begin to give attention to their words." And because "their words will be clothed with divine energy," unbelievers would "take knowledge of the Spirit whereby the Christians speak." So, "from admiring their lives, they will surely be led to consider and embrace their doctrine."[27] Effective mission and evangelism is not merely advanced by clever apologetics and other methods of persuasion. It is the Spirit-filled witness of transformed lives that makes the gospel both credible and compelling. Wesley concluded, "The holy lives of the Christians will be an argument they will not know how to resist."[28]

The truth of the gospel is made plausible by the living witness of authentic disciples, and is a necessary condition for the spread of the gospel. Nevertheless, we also need to recognize that people have the freedom to respond or resist the gospel, no matter how holy our lives or persuasive our words. Indeed, both Jesus and the early Methodists expected opposition and persecution as a result (Mt 5:10-11; Jn 15:18-19).

Finally, it is worth noting that Wesley illustrated his point by referring to the growth of the Methodist movement itself. From its small beginnings in the Holy Club at Oxford, "more and more saw the truth as it is in Jesus, and received it in the love thereof . . . It afterwards spread to every part of the land," and then to Ireland, America, and beyond.[29] These words also echo the Great Commission, given to an equally small group of zealous disciples with the mandate to make disciples of all nations. This could be the future for a small church or group of people who are ready to remember their baptism in discipleship and mission.

REMEMBERING OUR BAPTISM

To be a disciple is to "grow in the grace and knowledge of our Lord and Savior Jesus Christ" (2 Pet 3:18). The problem is that few churches expect to see this kind of change and growth among their members. To some extent, this lack of expectation is a self-fulfilling prophecy because the church does not offer the means needed for people to grow. Church leaders often end up maintaining communities of nominal Christians rather than raising up disciples as everyday missionaries. I suggest the most visible mark of cheap grace is found in churches that baptize people with no real intention of training them in discipleship and witness. But making disciples is not optional for a community called to participate in the mission of God. Here is what it might mean to remember our baptism and count the cost of disciple making as the church.[30]

- **Initiation into the life of discipleship**. We cannot settle for cheap grace, the assurance of conversion, or the benefits of church membership. Remembering our baptism in a post-Christendom world will involve the costly decision to adopt a way of life that is increasingly at odds with the prevailing culture. Such costly discipleship will be possible only through the life-transforming power of the Spirit who reminds us what Jesus taught so that our minds might be renewed and our lives conformed to his likeness. But are we willing to count the cost of doing whatever it takes to make discipleship our reason for being? Making disciples is rooted in a greater concern for promoting mission than preserving structures.

- **Dedication to the pursuit of holiness**. Wesley believed that the vocation of the early Methodist movement was not to make converts or church members but to spread scriptural holiness. As we will see, scriptural holiness is nothing more than the perfect love of God and neighbor. Remembering our baptism means seeking to become more like Jesus in mind, heart, and life. This requires a deep commitment to using the spiritual disciplines of piety and mercy as means of grace. But are we willing to count the cost of not settling for consumer-driven ministry? Making disciples is about equipping the saints for whole-life and lifelong discipleship.

- **Participation in the mission of God**. Engaging mission is not simply about the things we do, but concerns the kind of people we are. Being salt and light in the world means being filled, transformed, and overflowing with love of God and neighbor. Indeed, it can be argued that by pursuing the

Great Commandment, the Great Commission should take care of itself. Remembering our baptism will mean the pursuit of holiness because this is how we become missional by nature. But are we willing to count the cost of rejecting the sacred–secular divide? Making disciples will mean seeing our various forms of gathering as the means for celebrating, nurturing, and supporting the life of everyday missionaries.[31]

- **Collaboration in disciple-making fellowship**. Remembering our baptism means affirming that we cannot grow as mission-shaped disciples on our own. Living as a light in the world will engage us in spiritual warfare against the powers of darkness that lurk within our own hearts. That means embracing the kind of disciplined fellowship through which the remains of sin can be conquered and the reign of Jesus can be established throughout our lives. But are we willing to count the cost of resisting the temptation to find quick or easy solutions to disciple making? Making disciples takes the patient, slow, and demanding work of formation in discipleship and mission.

In the next chapter, we will start to develop these themes more fully by taking a closer look at what we mean by the life of discipleship as a journey of growth in grace and how we become co-workers with God in his mission of holy love.

QUESTIONS FOR GROUP DISCUSSION

1. After reading this chapter, how have your views about baptism and mission changed?
2. What do you find most inspiring about the brief history of mission presented here, and the Great Commission in particular?

3. How does the Great Commission apply to you personally in the twenty-first century? In what ways does this require you to count the cost of discipleship?

4. What are the challenges in thinking of yourself as an everyday missionary? How does your church equip you for the task?

5. Which parts of the fourfold pattern for remembering our baptism at the conclusion of this chapter do you find the most challenging? How is the Spirit guiding you?

CHAPTER 3

The Life of Discipleship

The God of grace . . . establish you and strengthen you by the power of the Holy Spirit, that you may live in grace and peace.[1]

Remembering our baptism means embracing the commitment to grow in the likeness of Jesus and to live in the power of his Spirit. Are you living consciously in the presence and power of God throughout everyday life?

Newly baptized Christians usually receive prayer for God to strengthen them in the life of discipleship that lies ahead. What often disappoints me, however, is the general lack of anything that conveys the expectation of growth in grace and its overflow in everyday mission.

There are many ways we could define the nature of discipleship, but we can start with the baptismal image of having new life through Christ. From this perspective, discipleship is first and foremost a way of life. The first disciples experienced this life in Jesus because he is the way, the truth, and the life (Jn 14:6-20). He is the way to the Father, because the Father lived and worked in him. He is the truth, because he did only what he saw the Father doing, and said only what he heard the Father saying. And he is the life, because he promised that the Father would raise him from the dead and send his life-giving Spirit to live in us. This is life, that we should have fellowship with God by following Jesus and being filled with his Spirit. Or to put it another way, the Spirit of truth guides our obedience to Jesus, and the life of God inhabits our faithful discipleship.

So here is another perspective on the Great Commission. We are called to make disciples, so they might have life-giving fellowship with the triune God (Jn 17:3; 1 Jn 3:15, 5:11-12). This is why we baptize people in the name of the Father, the Son, and the Holy Spirit. We teach them to obey the commands of Jesus because it is an invitation to share his way of life. The promise that lies behind all his teaching is that we might have the same relationship with the Father that he enjoyed and the same Spirit at work in our hearts that empowered his life. Following Jesus is not about slavish obedience but an opportunity to become like him in heart and life. Remembering our baptism means thinking of our commission as just that, a co-mission. The more we grow in the likeness of Jesus, the more we become co-workers in the mission of God.

THE MISSION OF GOD

Wesley did not use the language of "discipleship" as such, but he did speak about receiving new life in Christ as a "way" of salvation,[2] which is also the "way" to the kingdom of God.[3] So, we need to begin with the big story of God in Scripture and his mission of love to save a lost and broken world. Baptism reminds us that we are always first *recipients* of God's saving grace, so that we can become *participants* in his mission to save the world.

The God of Love, Life, and Light

The way of salvation is rooted in the concepts of repentance, faith, and holy living. These are found throughout the New Testament and especially in the writings of Paul, Peter, and James. But to understand who God is, and not just what he does, Wesley often turned to the gospel and letters of John, which get to "the foundation of all . . . the happy and holy communion which the faithful have with God the Father, Son, and Holy Ghost."[4]

In 1 John, we are told that God is love. From before the world began, God the Father has lived in a fellowship of love with the Son and the Spirit. From the perspective of Trinitarian theology, this means their love for each other is so intimate that they can only be thought of as three persons sharing one joyful life together. So also, God is life. The life they share is eternal life in the sense that it has no beginning or end and nothing can snuff it out. Finally, God is light. In the love and life of the triune God, there is no darkness at all. The persons of the Trinity have no self-centeredness, but give life to each other in the perfection of love (1 Jn 1:5, 4:8, 5:20).

Love, light, and life is revealed in Jesus, who is love made flesh, the light of the world, and the way to the Father. By receiving the gift of his Spirit, we are drawn into fellowship with the triune God (1 Jn 1:3). This fellowship empowers us to live as his children, to love one another, and to walk in the light. This is what it means to be baptized in the name of the Father, Son, and Holy Spirit.

Created for Life with God

The world was created as an expression of God's love, and the breath of God gave birth to Adam from lifeless dust. Adam was created in the image of God.[5] In Wesley's thinking, this made two

things possible. On the one hand, Adam had the capacity for relationship with God and could be drawn into fellowship with the
Father, Son, and Spirit. On the other hand, he had the capacity
to bear God's own nature and to reflect his love, life, and light in
the world.

Wesley explained that Adam enjoyed this fellowship with God
in three ways. First, his soul was created with spiritual senses that
enabled him to know God by experience. By them, Adam could
see God's presence, hear his voice, feel his embrace, taste his goodness, and even smell the fragrance of his company. Second, God
gave Adam holy desires, or character traits, that motivated him
to love and obedience. Filled with the life of God, his character
was ruled by love, joy, peace, and all the other fruit of the Spirit.
Finally, Adam was given freedom because God desires to be loved
freely in return. In Adam, all humanity inherits this promise of
life as the key to being holy and happy.[6] Baptism should remind
us that we were made for this life-giving and life-transforming fellowship with God.

Losing Our Lives to Sin

When the devil tempted Adam and Eve, his goal was to seduce
them away from their first love, to rob them of life, and cast a
shadow over their souls. He got them to act out of character by
exploiting their freedom to choose. We might surmise that the
Spirit within their hearts cried out, "Don't do it!" But they were
subtly deceived, and their seemingly small act of disobedience had
devastating consequences. The problem with sin is not just being
guilty of self-centeredness, but a broken relationship with God.
Wesley explained that the moment Adam took life into his own
hands, he died to God, "the most dreadful of all deaths." In doing
so, "he lost the life of God: He was separated from him, in union
with whom his spiritual life consisted."[7] The wages of sin is death.

God withdraws his living breath and Adam is one again perishable dust, having the form of a man but devoid of spiritual life. So now, in Adam, all human beings come into the world full of self-centeredness and are forced to live at odds with their true nature. Alienated from the life of God, we can walk the earth only as the living dead (Eph 2:12).[8] Baptism should remind us that we are free to choose, every day, whether we will live or die.

Living without God in the World

Wesley described how this loss of fellowship with God leads to brokenness within all the capacities of the soul. Sin lies like a veil over our spiritual senses, cutting us off from the light of God's presence. The more insensitive we become toward God, the more self-centeredness spreads like a virus throughout our whole character. The fruit of the Spirit is exchanged for the traits of a sinful nature. The apparent freedom of living for ourselves is really bondage to sin, and our fate is loneliness and despair. As the virus of sin spreads from person to person and place to place, all things become subject to decay in our hands. Adam's commission to take care of the earth was lost in the pursuit of self-interest. Baptism should remind us that we are predisposed toward self-centeredness by nature and need to be transformed in heart and life.

The Gift of New Life

When speaking about the fall of creation, Wesley meant the state of brokenness and spiritual death that comes from losing the life of God. In this condition, there is nothing we can do to heal ourselves. But "God so loved the world that he gave his one and only Son, so that whoever believes in him shall not perish but have eternal life" (Jn 3:16). Salvation comes through Jesus in two ways. First, he lays down his life for us as an atoning sacrifice so we might be forgiven and recover our life in God. This is what it means to be "justified." The Father heals our broken relationship through the death of his Son, by saving us from the guilt of sin and restoring our fellowship. Second, the risen Jesus baptizes us with his Spirit, so we might recover God's life in us and be transformed from the inside out. This is what it means to be "sanctified." The Father heals our fallen nature through the gift of his Spirit by saving us from the power of sin and renewing us in his image (Jn 1:29-33).

The purpose of Christ's coming was to destroy the works of the devil by restoring us to the life of God (1 Jn 3:8).[9] This means recovering the state that Adam enjoyed before the fall, when he was "unspeakably happy; dwelling in God, and God in him; having an uninterrupted fellowship with the Father and the Son, through the eternal Spirit."[10] In Adam, we all die. But in Christ, we are made alive again. Baptism should remind us that we all need the gift of new life.

Fullness of Life in Christ

Wesley called justification and sanctification the two "grand branches" of salvation. On the one hand, the Father sends Jesus into the world to live our life, die our death, and be raised again to bring us home. On the other hand, the Father sends the Spirit so we might follow in the way of Jesus, to die with him and be raised to new life as children of God. By the Spirit of adoption, we enter into the same relationship with God that Jesus had, as our hearts cry out, "Abba, Father." This inward witness brings an assurance of God's acceptance, so we can grow in the likeness of Jesus and be "conformed to the image of his Son" (Rom 8:14-17, 29). Discipleship is about having "Christ formed in the heart" (Gal 4:19),[11] so that we might "recover the life of God in your own soul, and walk as Christ walked" (1 Jn 2:6).[12]

New life in Christ is both inward and outward, but it flows from the inside out. First, our spiritual senses are opened and we are made "alive to God," so we may share in the same conscious fellowship with the Father that Jesus knew. Second, our character becomes changed into the likeness of Jesus, as the fruit of the Spirit takes root in our hearts. Third, this renovation of heart sets us free from the traits of self-centeredness, so our lives can be ruled by holy love of God and neighbor. Baptism should remind us that discipleship carries the promise of life in all its fullness.

The Overflow of Love and Life

In Wesley's thinking, the inward life of God cannot but be expressed in outward works of piety and mercy. The simplest summary of our fellowship with God is that we "rejoice always, pray continually, and give thanks in all circumstances; for this is God's will for you in Christ Jesus" (1 Thes 5:16-18). Thankful and joyful prayer is a heart "ever lifted up to God, at all times and in all places." For the one who has learned to pray without ceasing, "in retirement or company, in leisure, business, or conversation, his heart is ever with the Lord." And "whether he lie down or rise up, God is in all his thoughts; he walks with God continually, having the loving eye of his mind still fixed upon him, and everywhere 'seeing Him that is invisible.'"[13]

This loving communion with God overflows in love of neighbor. There is no piety without mercy. Every true disciple will seek to meet the needs of others, "and that in every possible kind; not only to their bodies . . . but much more does he labour to do good to their souls, as of the ability which God giveth; to awaken those that sleep in death; to bring those who are awakened to the atoning blood . . . and to provoke those who have peace with God to abound more in love and in good works . . . so they may 'all come unto the measure of the stature of the fullness of Christ.'"[14] Baptism should remind us that the life of discipleship is missional by nature.

The Final Victory of Life over Death

From this perspective, we might say the mission of God advances through disciples who are filled, transformed, and overflowing with his love, life, and light. The works of the devil are not merely destroyed in each person, but the gift of new life in Christ is spread from person to person and place to place. The commission of Adam to take care of the earth is restored by the Great Commission of Jesus to make disciples who share his mission of healing a broken world. For Wesley, the new creation is a vision of all humanity living in "an intimate, an uninterrupted union with God; a constant communion with the Father and his Son Jesus Christ, through the Spirit; a continual enjoyment of the Three–One God, and of all creatures in him."[15] This life is begun in the new birth and fulfilled in the new creation. The writer to the Hebrews explained, "We have tasted the goodness of the word of God and the powers of the coming age" (Heb 6:5). In the same way, Paul said, "If anyone is in Christ, the new creation has come: The old has gone, the new is here!" (2 Cor 5:17). Those who have the Spirit of adoption cry out "Abba, Father" and also groan, along with all creation, for God's purposes to be fulfilled (Rom 8:18-30). Baptism should remind us that salvation and discipleship are about being caught up in God's ultimate purposes for the renewal of all creation.[16]

A Journey of Grace and Faith

The idea that discipleship is sharing in the life of our triune God has ancient roots.[17] Irenaeus (202 CE) said, "The glory of God is man fully alive." He spoke of the Father as "restoring our spiritual union with him by his own 'two hands'—Jesus and God's life-giving Spirit."[18] With the one hand, God reaches out to us through the incarnation, life, death, and resurrection of Jesus. With the other hand, God draws us into fellowship with him as the indwelling Spirit enables us to participate in the way of salvation that Jesus has opened up. Salvation is entering this divine embrace, which "sets us free to live life as God intended, in union with the purposes of the Creator and Redeemer of the world."[19]

Discipleship is a journey of grace and faith in which we abide ever more deeply in fellowship with God, so we might participate ever more fully in the mission of God. From this perspective, we can think of "grace" as God reaching out to take hold of us with his love and our response of "faith" as simply surrendering ourselves to his transforming embrace. Let us explore the contours of this journey a bit more closely as we turn again to the teaching of Wesley.

God Seeks Us Irresistibly

God longs for us more than we ever long for him. He reaches out to us and actively pursues us with his love before we ever think about turning to him. The Spirit of the risen Jesus is at work in every human heart, whether we know it or not, whether we like it or not, and whether we feel worthy or not. "In him was life, and the life was the light of all people" (Jn 1:4, NRSV). Wesley called this "prevenient grace." The Spirit works through human conscience like a candle that draws a moth to the flame. He flickers over our drowsy spiritual senses and whispers in our ear, "Wake up, sleeper, rise from the dead, and Christ will shine on you" (Eph 5:14). The Spirit prepares our hearts for the good news of Jesus by drawing us to the shining beauty of his life. The first step of faith, by any awakened soul, is a decision to search out the promise of new life for oneself. God preveniently seeks us so that we might intentionally seek him. Baptism is a sign that the decision to follow Jesus is one that must be renewed every day.

God Embraces Us Unconditionally

The hands of the Father are always held out toward us, waiting for his children to reach back, so they can be lifted up and embraced. He does this unconditionally, for there is nothing we can do to deserve his love or take hold of him in our own strength. From the moment of our first awakening to the day we die, we turn to God only by surrendering ourselves to his embrace. Repentance means giving up every desire of the heart that holds us back and offering up every part of our lives into his hands. We come with empty hands of faith, trusting in the promise that God will accept us no matter who we are or the condition in which we come.

The gift of saving faith is truly knowing we are forgiven. When God embraces us, we know it. Justifying grace brings the conscious experience of God's embrace in which the Father whispers, "You are my child, and I delight in you," and the Spirit within our heart cries out, "Abba, Father!" In this embrace, there is new birth, adoption, intimacy, and growth in grace. Our identity as children of God is the heartbeat of discipleship. Repentance, faith, and forgiveness are the ways we enter and abide in his love. Baptism is a sign of justifying grace and our new identity in Christ.

God Changes Us Radically

The work of the Spirit is experienced as an abiding and transforming presence but also through inbreaking moments of revolutionary power. In these moments, we are not merely keeping in step with the Spirit but advancing in leaps and bounds. Wesley understood true conversion to be that moment when we experience the forgiveness of our sins and are born anew into a conscious relationship with God. This is what it means to enter the divine embrace; and our lives are never the same again.

Wesley emphasized the momentary nature of conversion to highlight how radically we are changed, not the manner in which it is accomplished or the amount of time it takes.[20] The radical nature of conversion is captured by the various images of baptism noted earlier: It is like passing from death to life and from darkness to light. To these, we might add new birth into the family of God. Wesley likened this radical change to natural childbirth. An unborn baby has lungs but does not breathe. It has senses but no immediate experience of the world. Similarly, the spiritually dead have souls that lack the breath of life and senses that are closed to the presence of God. But just as a baby is born in a "moment" to a whole new manner of living, so a disciple is born again into a whole new world and made alive to God. In that moment, the Spirit begins to renew the divine image in our souls. Our spiritual senses are opened; the love of God is shed abroad in our hearts; and our freedom from the tyranny of sin is secured.

Wesley explained that our new identity in Christ is sustained by "God's breathing into the soul, and the soul's breathing back what it first receives from God; a continual action of God upon the soul, and a reaction of the soul upon God; an unceasing presence of God, the loving, pardoning God, manifested to the heart, and perceived by faith; and an unceasing return of love, praise, and prayer, offering up all the thoughts of our hearts, all the words of our tongues, all the works of our hands, all our body, soul, and spirit, to be a holy sacrifice, acceptable unto God in Christ Jesus."[21] Baptism is a sign of sanctifying grace, the new birth, and the call to grow in our identity as children of God.

God Transforms Us Gradually

For Wesley, being forgiven and born again is still only half the gospel. It is but a moment in the movement of the Spirit in our lives.

The destiny of a newborn baby is growing up to maturity. So too, living in the embrace of God's love is an invitation to grow as his children, in the likeness of his Son. By his sanctifying grace, we grow into the character of Jesus through the fruit of his Spirit, and we grow in the ministry of Jesus through the gifts of his Spirit. Salvation is not mere conversion but sanctification, or being set apart for this Spirit-filled and Jesus-shaped way of life.

The gift of new birth comes in a moment, but growth in grace takes a lifetime to receive. Wesley noted that the Spirit draws us into "fellowship with the Father and the Son," and "by a kind of spiritual respiration . . . the child of God grows up, till he comes to the 'full measure of the stature of Christ'."[22] The divine embrace becomes a working relationship with the Spirit as we seek to grow through the means of grace in prayer, searching the Scriptures, fasting or abstinence, the Lord's Supper, and works of mercy.

Being intentional in our pursuit of holiness is not an optional extra for serious disciples. Wesley said, "If we do not then love him who first loved us; if we will not hearken to his voice; if we turn our eye away from him, and will not attend to the light which he pours upon us; his Spirit will not always strive: He will gradually withdraw, and leave us to the darkness of our own hearts. He will not continue to breathe into our soul, unless our soul breathes toward him again."[23] Baptism is a sign of our commitment to stay connected to the life-transforming power of God, which comes through the means of grace.

God Perfects Us Completely

Wesley claimed that God raised up the Methodist movement to spread scriptural holiness over the land. He also believed that the doctrine of "Christian perfection" was "the *grand depositum*" that God had entrusted them to proclaim. In short, God had set them apart and sent them out to invite all people into a journey of faith marked by holiness of heart and life with the goal of perfect love.

For many, the very word "holiness" is enough to strike fear into the heart, and the idea of "perfection" does not do much for them either! We are right to be wary of perfectionism. But Wesley spoke of perfection as the spiritual maturity we are called to throughout Scripture and by the ancient traditions of the church (*teleios* in Greek, translated as *perfectio* in Latin).[24] This life is best described as "perfection in love"; that is, seeking a life that is completely filled, transformed, and overflowing with holy love of God and neighbor. It is something we are to seek because it is something God has promised and longs to give.

Like the new birth, Wesley believed perfect love was a radical change that the Spirit could complete in a moment. This teaching has led to much controversy, which we will look at later. For now, it is enough to note that authentic discipleship is determined not by whether we have attained the goal but by whether we are striving after it. Baptism is a sign of our longing for more of God and a confidence that he will fulfill his promises by finishing what he started in our conversion.

CO-WORKERS IN THE GOSPEL

Wesley does not use the terminology of "mission," but he does speak about "the work of God" to lead humanity through this way of salvation. We are called to be "co-workers with God" in the journey of discipleship and in his mission to a lost and broken world. The moment of baptism immerses us into the movement of the Spirit in the following three ways.

Working out Our Salvation

In Philippians 2, Paul instructs us to have the mind of Christ and to follow Jesus' example of loving service. We become like him by working out our own salvation with fear and trembling as the Spirit enables us "to will and to work for his good pleasure." This is how we are to live and grow as children of God, who "shine like stars in the world" (Phil 2:5-12, 15).

Wesley said we become co-workers with God because the Spirit of life "breathes into us every good desire, and brings every good desire to good effect."[25] Indeed, God is always at work in our hearts, leading and moving us into action. He said, "There is no man, unless he has quenched the Spirit, that is wholly void of the grace of God."[26] The question is not whether God is at work in us, but whether we will follow the movements of his Spirit in our hearts. We must work out our salvation with "utmost earnestness of spirit" because failure to follow is not an option. Following the Spirit means breathing in and out through works of piety and mercy. Our lives are sustained by this spiritual respiration. Breathe or die. Grow or die. Serve or die. In baptism, we pledge to work out our own salvation.

Living as God's Handiwork

Paul also said, "We are God's handiwork, created in Christ Jesus to do good works, which God prepared in advance for us to do" (Eph 2:10). These are the works that Jesus did and set as an example for his disciples to follow. Works of piety include prayer and fasting; and prayerful works of mercy include feeding the hungry, giving drink to the thirsty, clothing the naked, relieving the stranger, and visiting those who are sick and in prison (Mt 25:35-36). He also thinks about evangelistic activities as works of mercy for the soul, as we "contribute in any manner to the saving of souls from death."[27]

Again, living as the handiwork of God is not an option for our discipleship. Wesley warned, "The walking herein is essentially necessary, as to the continuance of that faith whereby we are already saved by grace."[28] This is because we are always co-working with some "spirit" or other. If we are not intentionally working together with the Holy Spirit as children of God, then we will unintentionally become co-workers with the spirit of worldliness as children of the devil.[29] In baptism, we pledge to resist the temptation to partner with the works of evil by becoming a co-worker with God.

Co-Working in God's Service

Finally, those who are called to leadership become "co-workers in God's service" through the activity of sowing, planting, and watering the gospel in people's lives (1 Cor 3:5-9). This means urging them "not to receive God's grace in vain" (2 Cor 6:1-2). We cannot settle for making converts who are not true disciples, or Christians without a commitment to Christ-likeness, or followers of Jesus who do not get caught up in his disciple-making mission. The early Methodist preachers were frequently observed to have "the work of God at heart," which overflowed in a zeal for promoting the work of God in the hearts of others.[30] To some extent, as we shall see, this vocation belongs to every disciple. In baptism, we pledge to help others work out their own salvation with fear and trembling.

REMEMBERING OUR BAPTISM

Let us draw the threads of this big story together to see how the life of discipleship connects baptism and mission. To do this, we will also adopt Wesley's way of asking questions for reflection and self-examination.

- **Initiation into the life of discipleship**. For Wesley, authentic discipleship flows from the life of God in the soul. It is a daily communion with the Father, through the Son, in the power of the Spirit. This life is expressed in works of piety and mercy, and is nurtured by them. But these are means of grace not ends in themselves. Remembering our baptism will keep us mindful that neither the inner nor the outer life of discipleship is optional, but it is the life of God in the soul that must be pursued above all else. The renewal of discipleship or revitalization of the church can come only from the gift of new life. Unless this is our goal, all our practices and programs will be futile. Ask yourself: "Do I have the gift of new life? Do I know the forgiving embrace of God? Can I sense the fruit of the Spirit growing in my heart and life? Am I growing in grace through works of piety and mercy? Am I committed to working out my salvation with fear and trembling?"

- **Dedication to the pursuit of holiness**. We cannot settle for just being converts or church members, because the pursuit of holiness is not optional for discipleship. Without it, our lives will eventually be reduced to the mere form of religion, lacking the power of godliness. Without intentional discipleship, newborn converts will die, and nominal church members will never truly live. Remembering our baptism will convince us of the need to become like Jesus so that the love, life, and light of God can be made visible in the world. The gracious hands of God that embrace us also reach out through us to embrace others, as his love is made tangible in our witness and service. Ask yourself: "Am I becoming more like Jesus? Do I have a heart for lifeless and broken people? Do I intend to follow the impulses of the Spirit, to love and serve those in need, both body and soul? Is my life an example worth following? One that can lead others into the way of life?"

- **Participation in the mission of God**. This happens in two ways. First, we must become *recipients* of his saving grace so we might be filled and transformed by his love, life, and light. Second, we then become *participants* in mission, as our lives are transformed and overflowing with love of God and neighbor. Remembering our baptism will challenge us to freely give what we have freely received. It will also convict us that we cannot give to others what we have not received for ourselves. So, living as everyday missionaries requires us to be intentional about seeking God for both his justifying and sanctifying grace. Unless we enter the divine embrace and abide deeply with God, we cannot draw others to him or live missionally in the world. Ask yourself: "Do I have this life in me that God wants others to receive? Am I abiding deeply with God in prayer so others might be drawn to his presence in me? Am I serving others in word and deed so they might be connected with the love and life of God? Do I desire to be a co-worker with God in the salvation of others?"

- **Collaboration in disciple-making fellowship**. We cannot pursue the journey of discipleship and mission alone. We need the accountability and guidance of spiritual friends who will help us seek those moments of blessing that come from the inbreaking power of the Spirit. We also need them to prevent us from settling for the moments of blessing by encouraging us to follow the daily movements of the Spirit, so we might abound in love and good works. Ask yourself: "Do I have spiritual friends who share my life deeply and help me walk more closely with God, day by day? Do they know me well enough to help me discern the movements of the Spirit in my heart and life? Are they familiar enough with my strengths and weaknesses to help me follow his lead as a faithful follower of Jesus?"

In the next chapter, we will look more closely at the connection between baptism and conversion in the life of discipleship.

QUESTIONS FOR GROUP DISCUSSION

1. After reading this chapter, how have your views changed about salvation and the gift of new life?
2. How would you summarize the saving mission of God? What difference does it make to think of mission as belonging to God and not to us?
3. In what ways is it helpful to think of salvation as a journey from awakening to perfection? At what point do you think our journey of grace and faith usually stalls? What can be done about it?
4. What does it mean to be a co-worker with God? Why do you think God wants us to become co-workers with him in our own salvation and in his mission to the world?
5. Which parts of the fourfold pattern for remembering our baptism at the conclusion of this chapter do you find the most challenging? How is the Spirit guiding you?

CHAPTER 4

The Paradox of Conversion

*Through the Sacrament of Baptism . . . we are incorporated into
God's mighty acts of salvation and given new birth through water
and the Spirit.*[1]

Remembering our baptism means enjoying the privilege of
living as a child of God and being saved to the uttermost.
Are you assured of your identity in Christ and growing in
his likeness through the power of his Spirit?

The promise of new birth reminds us of the answer Jesus gave
to Nicodemus about how to inherit the kingdom: "Very truly
I tell you, no one can see the kingdom of God unless they are born
of water and the Spirit" (John 3:5). Nicodemus was confused by
the command to be "born again"; not because he didn't understand Jesus, but because he knew exactly what it meant! It was a
term associated with the conversion of gentiles to Judaism. As the
gentiles lived and worked alongside the Jews, some were attracted
by their life and faith and expressed the desire to become a part of
the Jewish community. The rite of initiation included baptism in
water as a sign of repentance from false religions, then receiving
the mark of circumcision as a sign of belonging to the covenant

people. After baptism, a gentile was considered to be reborn as a radically new person. All ties to his previous life were broken, and he was adopted into the family of God.[2]

As a teacher of Israel, Nicodemus would have known all this. It was simply unthinkable that Jesus might have compared him to an unconverted gentile! Yet this is exactly what Jesus did. He was founding a renewal movement within the bounds of Judaism as a way of recalling the people of God to their true identity as light of the world. Even for those who had been raised as children of Abraham, this would take nothing less than rebirth, a fresh baptism in water and the Spirit. The movement of Jesus would be the common means by which all people, Jew and gentile alike, entered into the kingdom of God.

God has continued to raise up renewal movements throughout the history of the church whenever it has lost sight of the Great Commission. Early Methodism was one such movement, situated within a spiritually lukewarm Church of England.[3] Like Jesus, Wesley preached a message of new birth within the religious institution of his time; and like Nicodemus, respectable baptized members of the church found it difficult to understand why they needed to be born again. In this chapter, we will explore this paradox in order to see how the moment of baptism relates to a movement of renewal. In doing so, remembering our baptism will confront us with the need to rediscover our true identity as the children of God if the church is to renew its mission of making disciples.

THE JOURNEY OF CONVERSION

John Wesley encouraged his preachers to keep journals and then distill them into autobiographies for publication. These stories typically included an account of their conversion and subsequent spiritual journey as disciples and co-workers in the gospel.[4] Wesley intended them to illustrate his teaching on the way of salvation and the connections between conversion, discipleship, and mission.[5]

Unlike some traditions of autobiography, these stories are not presented in the form of heroic tales or romantic ideals, which can be dismissed as unattainable in everyday life. Rather, they are realistic testimonies of how God transforms the lives of ordinary Christians and empowers them for service. Although their stories are quite varied, it is possible to identify a common journey of conversion.[6]

Awakening

These autobiographies were written from within the Christendom context of eighteenth-century England. Not everyone went to church, but they were all schooled in a culture shaped by biblical stories and gospel values. It was also a time without the comforts of modern life or healthcare. Commonplace illnesses could end someone's life at any age, and a large percentage of babies died before the age of one. Families lived close to the edge of eternity, and the fear of death was an ever-present theme. They absorbed the dominant religious imperative to live good lives in order to avoid hell. So, it is not altogether surprising that many stories of conversion begin with experiences of prevenient grace as very young children. The Spirit would implant a variety of inclinations and desires after godliness, and they grew up with an inner spiritual struggle against the temptations of worldly life.

This struggle went unresolved until they came across the witness of a friend or co-worker who had been caught up in the Methodist movement. They would often be invited to hear a preacher and encountered the message, "You must be born again." The new birth was a doorway to the pursuit of holiness, without which there could be no happiness in this life or the next. Only the perfect love of God shed abroad in the heart by the Spirit can cast out the fear of death. Only a conscious assurance of forgiveness brings peace with God and the power to overcome sin. And only a life devoted to the love of God and neighbor can put an end to the spiritual battle within every restless heart. This good news was both confusing and compelling at the same time. For those who were already baptized as infants, it was hard to hear a message that they still needed to be born again. Yet, once awakened to the promises of God, they were left longing for more.

Longing

There was something different about the early Methodist witness. Wesley criticized so-called "gospel preachers" who peddled a message of easy conversion without the call to discipleship.[7] He insisted that preaching the grace of Christ must be accompanied by proclaiming the law of Christ and the pursuit of holiness. The good news is not merely that we can be forgiven our sins but our hearts and lives can be renewed in the image of God. The purpose of sharing the whole gospel, whether in sermons or conversations, was to cast a vision for fullness of life in Christ and stir up a spiritual appetite that could not be spoiled by cheap grace.

The early Methodists often sang about their longing for more of God, but only through a veil of sin and unbelief. They are blind, but long to see God face-to-face; deaf, but long to hear a word that raises the dead; hard of heart, but long to feel the embrace of forgiving love and taste the goodness of God.[8] Their prayerful souls would groan and gasp for the breath of life, mourn and cry for the comforting witness of sins forgiven, hunger and thirst for the righteousness of new birth.[9] Awakening was not merely a fleeting curiosity in spiritual things, but a deep work of the Spirit that captivated their imaginations and made them "prisoners of the gospel."

Seeking

One frequent reason given for slow spiritual progress toward conversion was the lack of a shepherd or spiritual guide. In the midst of revival, these so-called gospel preachers invited people to make decisions of faith but then abandoned them to the care of the local church. Unfortunately, the local churches were neither hospitable toward these seekers nor spiritually equipped to help them grow as disciples.

Evangelism in the early Methodist movement was subtly different. Awakened seekers were not led through a sinner's prayer or just sent to church. Rather, they were invited to join Methodist societies and incorporated into class meetings where they helped one another seek the experience of evangelical conversion.[10] When people did experience new birth, they were encouraged to embrace the added intimacy of band meetings as a means for pressing on to perfection. More will be said about this in chapter seven.

Long experience enabled Wesley to observe an ordinary pattern in the journey of conversion. The awakened seeker "begins searching the Scriptures" and praying to God with other believers. "Thus he continues in God's way, in hearing, reading, meditating, praying, and partaking of the Lord's Supper, till God, in the manner that pleases Him, speaks to his heart."[11] In the class meeting, leaders would guide them in using the means of grace according to each one's particular needs. Wesley described how class leaders must "work together with God" to "second the motions of the blessed Spirit." He continued, "The means into which different men are led, and in which they find the blessing of God, are varied, transposed, and combined together a thousand different ways . . . for who knows in which God will meet thee with the grace that bringeth salvation?"[12]

Birthing

It could take up to two years of participation in a Methodist society before a seeker would come to the experience of new birth.[13] The journey of discipleship, shaped by works of piety and mercy, was training in the art of repentance. They cultivated a deeper longing for holiness and a growing expectation of inbreaking grace. The season of searching was often marked by two kinds of spiritual experience. On the one hand, the Spirit would grant them tangible foretastes of saving grace. This included a sense of God's desire to forgive, to set them free from fear, to overcome the power of sin, and to rule their hearts with holy love. These moments of revelation led to resolutions for pressing on toward the prize. On the other hand, daily life presented many unexpected moments of spiritual crisis, in which the truth of God's promises could be tested. These crises came in the form of besetting sins, personal sicknesses, or grief over the death of loved ones. Sometimes, it was the loss of a newborn baby or a small child.

These foretastes of heaven and crises of conscience provided opportunities for a greater abandonment to God and dedication to his ways. But seekers often found themselves caught in a cycle of godly conviction and practical resolution, then lapsing into temptation and spiritual dissipation. They often used the language of spiritual warfare to describe this battle in their souls. In fellowship with others, they waited on God in the means of grace and wrestled with God through prayer. These small groups became wombs of new birth in which the members served as midwives. What marked the moment of conversion was a sense that the cycle of breakthrough and backsliding was finally broken. This was accompanied by an abiding assurance of being embraced by God's love that endured through the trials and temptations of life to follow. Ultimately, though, the mark of true conversion was an unwavering dedication to the pursuit of holiness.

You Must Be Born Again

The message of conversion and new birth presented a problem for the Church of England's teaching on baptism. Although there has been some speculation about whether Wesley changed his mind over time, it is reasonably clear that he accepted the practice of infant baptism as a faithful Anglican clergyman and repeated the received wisdom of the church with little adaptation.[14] This included the idea of infant regeneration, which meant that the gift of new birth was imparted through administration of the sacrament itself.

Nevertheless, Wesley's primary concern was more apostolic. His energies were spent in calling both churched and unchurched people to the experience of new birth as a foundation for the pursuit of holiness. Because of this, the presence of Methodism as an evangelical movement created a paradox of conversion within the church. Incorporation into the parish was through the regenerating waters of infant baptism, while incorporation into the Methodist movement was marked by a desire for new birth among those who were already baptized.[15]

Living Answerable to Our Baptism

Some of those who heard Wesley's message of evangelical conversion turned to remembering their baptism as a way of dodging the draft. He noted how some might reason "he was born again in baptism. Therefore he cannot be born again now." Regardless of what may have happened in the past, Wesley drew attention to their present spiritual condition: "Alas, what trifling is this! What, if he was then a child of God? He is now manifestly a child of the devil."[16] Others objected that his doctrine of the new birth was tantamount to denying one's baptism. In response, Wesley did not mince his words: "Was you devoted to God at eight days old, and have you been all these years devoting yourself to the devil?" He continued, "You have already denied your baptism" with every willful sin. So, "deny whatever thou pleasest, but deny not this; let me be 'born from above!'"[17]

Ultimately, Wesley argued that the benefit of infant baptism remains only "if we live answerable thereto; if we repent, believe, and obey the gospel."[18] Reflecting on his own experience at Aldersgate, he noted, "I believe, till I was about ten years old I had not sinned away that 'washing of the Holy Ghost' which was given me in baptism."[19] Indeed, he assumed that most other people had "sinned away" or "denied" their baptism, requiring a fresh experience of God's converting grace and a fresh personal response of committed discipleship. So he urged all his hearers to "lean no more on the staff of that broken reed, that ye were born again in baptism." Rather, he exhorts them to "receive again what they have lost, even the 'Spirit of adoption, crying in their hearts, Abba, Father!'"[20]

Wesley's logic certainly reminds us that whether we have been baptized as infants or adult believers, the ever-present danger is that we will sin away the grace of new birth. In other words, we may become so unresponsive to the Spirit in our lives that we lose the conscious identity of being the children of God. Remembering our baptism, as individuals and churches, is a matter of accountability for the life of discipleship.[21]

Baptism as a Way of Life

Wesley tried to maintain the paradox of infant baptism and evangelical conversion by giving them different roles in the way of salvation. On the one hand, infant baptism represents the enduring promise of prevenient grace and the possibility of repentance and faith. This comes through incorporation into the church and the covenant of grace. On the other hand, the call for evangelical conversion and discipleship represents the need for our dynamic response to God's saving grace and covenanting initiative. This recognizes our perpetual need for repentance and faith for the pursuit of holiness.

Like entering the covenant of marriage, the moment of baptism involves a lifelong commitment with vows that must be remembered and promises that wait to be fulfilled. This means that baptism, like marriage, is also a way of life. Whether we are baptized as infants or through personal decision, fulfilling this baptismal covenant needs the dynamic response of mutual love, so that our relationship with God may grow and deepen over time. Since God is utterly faithful, the covenant relationship will be compromised only through our own self-centeredness. We may sin away our baptism by giving our hearts to worldliness, which is, in effect, a form of spiritual adultery.

Living with the Paradox

With the transition from discipleship movement to institutional church, the history of Methodism has had to reckon with the paradox of conversion within its own structures. The overarching challenge has been maintaining the evangelical character of discipleship with the normativity of infant baptism.[22] On the one hand, an overemphasis on the enduring promise of God's grace tends to compromise the evangelical impulse toward seeking new life, which is necessary for church renewal. When this happens, remembering our baptism gets reduced to a celebration of prevenient grace and discipleship gets equated with church membership. On the other hand, overemphasizing our dynamic response to God's grace can make too much of our own efforts or decisions and compromise the full inclusion of children in the covenant. When this happens, remembering our baptism can be reduced to celebrating bygone moments of conversion, even as our discipleship slides into various shades of cheap grace.

We can live with the paradox only by remembering that baptism is a mark of new birth as well as the life of discipleship that flows from it. One factor that continues to eclipse this fuller meaning of baptism is the problem of individualism and our preference for privatized spirituality. It is no coincidence that the transition of Methodism from movement to church also led to the decline of class and band meetings. The majority of Methodist churches today generally lack these practices of discipleship, and remembering the enduring promises of infant baptism can all too easily become a substitute for personal conversion.

MARKING THE GIFT OF NEW LIFE

The evangelistic outcome of disciple-making mission is that unbelievers will repent and be baptized. Repentance is a turning away from the old life of sin, and baptism is an initiation into the new life of discipleship. This is the normative pattern of conversion in Scripture established by the first disciples as they carried out the Great Commission. It is clearly repeated in the baptism of adult converts. The problem comes when God begins to re-evangelize the church by raising up movements of renewal, especially in contexts where infant baptism has been a longstanding practice. In these cases, the question is, "How do we mark the experience of conversion among those who are already baptized, and usually as infants?"

Evangelizing the Baptized

Wesley was caught on the horns of a dilemma. On the one hand, he belonged to a church that baptized everyone but wasn't making disciples. On the other hand, he was the founder of a disciple-making movement that couldn't baptize most of its converts. We will begin to tease out this dilemma by examining Wesley's practice of adult baptism.[23]

First, as a faithful high-churchman, Wesley was open to the possibility that baptism could be a means of regeneration. Prior to the founding of the first Methodist society, he baptized repentant seekers, hoping they would receive the gift of new birth. But without disciplined fellowship, such baptisms did not bear fruit. After the introduction of class meetings, however, Wesley started baptizing those who were already working out their salvation and reported how frequently the means of grace proved to be effective.

Second, as an evangelical leader, Wesley came to distinguish between the rite of baptism and the experience of conversion. Just as baptism did not always lead to new birth, he observed that people could be born again without having been baptized. Wesley still insisted on water baptism in obedience to the command of Jesus and the example of Scripture (Acts 10:47).

But what should be done to mark the conversion of those who had already been baptized? Wesley's answer to the paradox came in the form of visible commitment to the discipline of Christian fellowship. One mark was participation in class meetings where seekers became converts and converts became co-workers in the salvation of other seekers. A second mark was the incorporation of those who experienced new birth into band meetings, where they helped one another press on to perfection. A third mark was the practice of covenant renewal, which was an annual event in early Methodism but also woven into the rhythms of everyday discipleship. This will be the main theme of our next chapter.

The Problem with Confirmation

One way the historic church has addressed the paradox of conversion is through the practice of confirmation. This provides a means for tying together the covenant promises made on behalf of an infant with the subsequent response of personal faith. But the practice of confirmation has many ambiguities of its own. Understanding them will require a very brief history of the practice.

The early church looked to the baptism of Jesus himself as an example to follow. On the one hand, Jesus was baptized in water, which marked his identification with the people of God and the history of salvation. On the other hand, he was also baptized in the Spirit, which marked his identity as the Son of God and anointed him with power and authority to fulfill his calling. Following this pattern, new converts were immersed in water as a sign of participation in the death and resurrection of Jesus. This was followed by anointing with oil and the laying on of hands to "confirm" the saving grace of God with the gift of the Spirit. Baptism and confirmation were united in a single rite of initiation.

After the conversion of Emperor Constantine and in the evolution of Christendom, this pattern began to change. When Christianity was imposed as the religion of the state, infant baptism started to become normative and became largely a mark of good citizenship. As Christianity spread across the empire, church government increasingly regulated the rite of baptism. Parish priests were allowed to baptize people with water, but the bishops alone reserved the right to confirm them by the laying on of hands. With the growth of the church, however, the relative scarcity of bishops meant infants were being baptized without the opportunity for confirmation. So, for quite pragmatic reasons, confirmation was separated from baptism and became a subsequent rite for young adults to complete what happened at infancy. Today, the practice of confirmation in many local churches has been reduced to a rite of membership and has lost the charismatic dimension of baptism in the Spirit.[24] This will be the theme of chapter nine.

As a faithful high churchman, Wesley claimed to uphold all the rites of the church, including that of confirmation. As an evangelical leader, however, he was essentially silent on the issue of confirmation. When the Methodist movement became a denominational church in America, Wesley prepared *The Sunday Service* as a standard of liturgy. He intentionally removed any indication that the new birth was a necessary outcome of baptism and removed the rite of confirmation altogether. Ultimately, it appears that Wesley thought confirmation was irrelevant. This may have been true while the church retained the character of an evangelical movement whose members intentionally sought the life-transforming gift of the Spirit. In other words, the rite of confirmation should be unnecessary in a community that is fulfilling its commission to make Spirit-filled and Jesus-shaped disciples. But what happens when the spirit of a movement is lost?

The Post-Christendom Challenge

I am a third generation unchurched convert. I did not darken the door of a church until my late teens, when a cousin started sharing his newfound faith with me. I really knew nothing of the gospel and was easy prey for prevenient grace! As a budding scientist, my journey of faith just seemed like an exciting adventure into a supernatural world that I had never considered before. Over time, Christian friends helped me learn how to read my Bible and pray. Then one day, in my first year of studying biochemistry at the university, the Spirit convinced me that I was a child of God while I was writing a lab report at my desk. I remember joyfully offering up my life to God. Since then, I have had my heart strangely warmed more than once. I cannot give you the dates or times because no one told me it was important to log them. But I have zealously pursued the life of discipleship, and it has been a wonderful journey.

I was attending an evangelical Anglican church in London at the time of my conversion and decided to get baptized as a public declaration of my faith. When they asked if I had already been baptized, I did not know the answer. My parents proudly affirmed that I was "christened" as an infant, and they had celebrated my birth in the traditional way. I was thoroughly disappointed and even angry. They had me baptized when they were not Christians themselves and had no intention of raising me as a disciple. I agreed to be confirmed, though it seemed like a consolation prize at the time. Since then, I have come to see confirmation as a sign that my parents had given me up to God in baptism, and he was fulfilling his promises in my life. Even so, there was no anointing with oil, and I don't remember any charismatic prayer. It would be another couple of years before baptism in the Spirit would become a reality for me. My mother became a disciple shortly after my confirmation, and my father properly confessed his faith through his struggle with dementia.

I grew up in a generation when infant baptism was still culturally normal, even though the culture itself was becoming increasingly out of touch with the gospel. Our situation today is being referred to as "post-Christendom" and even "post-Christian," insofar as the vast majority of people have neither heard nor responded to the gospel, despite there being a church building on every street corner. Unlike in the time of Wesley, the average person today will most likely belong to the unbaptized masses of humanity. If the church earnestly seeks to fulfill the Great Commission and the practice of believer's baptism becomes the normal heartbeat of our ministry again, the paradox created by infant baptism and subsequent conversion will be greatly diminished. Somewhat like the time of Wesley, however, the paradox will remain in churches that practice infant baptism, even if it is reserved for the children of believing parents. One way or another, there will be a need to mark the experience of conversion among the already baptized as the personal decision to become a follower of Jesus.

Perhaps there is room for a more substantial practice of confirmation as an occasion for remembering our baptism in water and seeking baptism in the Spirit.[25] This was certainly the experience of Hannah Ball, an early Methodist leader, who noted in her memoir, "It has been my privilege this day to be confirmed . . . I am persuaded that many members of our Society have quenched the Spirit by not submitting to the order of confirmation. I earnestly pray for a fresh confirmation of the work of God in my heart, that the fruits of the Spirit may be manifested in my life."[26]

Of course, a simple answer would be to ditch the practice of infant baptism altogether. But there is still too much to commend it as a sign of prevenient and covenanting grace, as we shall see.[27] Perhaps we can envision infant and believer's baptism as two distinct and complementary rites. For example, maybe we could think of one baptism in two parts, begun as an infant and completed in confirmation.[28] One of the most creative approaches I have seen was developed by a joint Anglican-Baptist community, which offers confirmation by immersion in water.[29] Either way, from a Wesleyan perspective, it matters little when and how people are baptized if the pursuit of holiness and whole-life and life-long discipleship is not the primary mark of our conversion.

REMEMBERING OUR BAPTISM

I will now draw together these reflections on conversion and discipleship to see how they might shape our thinking about baptism and the practice of remembrance.

- **Initiation into the life of discipleship.** Taking the Wesleyan tradition seriously will not let us settle for either nominal Christianity or cheap grace. If baptism is a mark of conversion and discipleship, remembering our baptism must lead to robust accountability rather than easy assurances. Regardless of whether we were once baptized as infants or adults, the question is: "Are we now born again, and do we have the witness of the Spirit abiding in our hearts?" Baptism may well be an incorporation into church membership, but there can be no membership of the kingdom without personal repentance and faith. We may be able to date a past experience of conversion, but the mark of true conversion is the daily life of discipleship. Remembering our baptism should be a means of celebrating the enduring nature of God's grace, but it is also a means of reflecting on the grace we may have known and lost, or have yet to experience in the first place.[30]

- **Dedication to the pursuit of holiness**. Following the example of Jesus, we cannot settle for being baptized merely with water. If baptism is a mark of conversion and transformation, remembering our baptism will also inspire us to seek baptism in the Spirit. Even if our hearts have been strangely warmed in the past, the questions are: "Are we seeking the fullness of the Spirit day by day (Eph 5:18)? Does the Spirit bear witness with our spirit that we are children of God, growing more like Jesus in heart and life?" Baptism is a sign of God's enduring love and forgiveness of our sins, but it should also be a sign of the Spirit's dynamic and life-transforming presence in our hearts. Remembering our baptism must take us beyond the confines of guilt management and into the glory of growing as Spirit-filled disciples.

- **Participation in the mission of God**. The pursuit of discipleship is not merely about personal salvation. Remembering our baptism will challenge us to work out our own salvation to become co-workers with God in the salvation of others. Only as we become recipients of his life-transforming grace can we become participants in his world-changing mission. As we serve those outside the church, the questions are: "Do we see them as candidates for baptism? Do we aspire for them to know God's saving grace and come to the new birth for themselves?" The aim of any baptizing church must be more than making members or even converts, but nurturing whole-life and lifelong followers of Jesus.

- **Collaboration with disciple-making fellowship**. Baptism may be a mark of incorporation into the church, but remembering our baptism will mean reflecting on whether our practices of Christian fellowship are adequate to help people grow in the journey of discipleship. We must ask: "Who helps us overcome the spirit of condemnation at work within our hearts and discover the unconditional love of God? Who helps us overcome the spirit of worldliness at work in our lives and discover the power of God to set us free from temptation? Who helps us overcome the spirit of self-centeredness and discover the blessedness of sharing God's love with our neighbor in word and deed?" Without the fellowship of others, we are too easily tempted to sin away our baptism.

In the next chapter, we will look more closely at the Wesleyan practice of covenant renewal, and we shall see how this becomes a dynamic response to the enduring nature of God's covenanting grace. It will remind us that baptism is a way of life, and the decision to follow Jesus must be made every day.

Questions for Group Discussion

1. After reading this chapter, how have your views changed about conversion and discipleship?
2. What difference does it make to think about conversion as a moment in time or as a process over time? Can these two ways of thinking be integrated?
3. How would you explain what it means to be born again? Why do you think Wesley was so insistent that Christians must be

born again, even if they were already baptized? In what ways is this a challenge to your church?

4. Have you been baptized or confirmed as a believer? If so, what did it mean for you at the time? What promises did you make, and what kinds of prayers were said over you?

5. Which parts of the fourfold pattern for remembering our baptism at the conclusion of this chapter do you find the most challenging? How is the Spirit guiding you?

CHAPTER 5

The Practice of Covenant Renewal

Through the reaffirmation of our faith, we renew the covenant declared at our baptism, acknowledge what God is doing for us, and affirm our commitment to Christ's holy Church.[1]

Remembering our baptism means giving our whole lives to God in response to the gift of his own life to us. Are you living as though all you think, feel, speak, and do is for God and his kingdom?

At services of baptism, the congregation may be provided with an opportunity to reaffirm their faith. Remembrance starts with holding fast to our place in the covenant and our identity as children of God. This is good, but there is a danger that it can easily become a nostalgic reminder of God's unconditional grace or a sentimental assurance of his forgiving love that really does not change our everyday lives. The real question is not whether *God is for us* but whether *we are for God*. The true goal of remembrance is renewing our commitment to live as good stewards of the love and grace we have received. God constantly goes before us, and we are invited to take steps of obedient faith. God constantly reaches out to forgive our sins, and we are invited to turn back to him in repentance. God constantly works within us, and we are invited to work out our salvation with fear and trembling. The invitation is unchanging, but how will we respond?

This relationship of gracious promise and faithful response is symbolized by the covenant first made between God and Abraham, then with his people Israel, and now with his new community the church. Paul reminds the gentile converts in Ephesus that they were once "excluded from citizenship in Israel and foreigners to the covenants of the promise, without hope and without God in the world" (Eph 2:12). The good news is that God has made a way for all people to enter the covenant through Christ and sealed this relationship with the gift of the Spirit. Baptism is the sign of our inclusion in the covenant and our commitment to live as his holy people.

Nevertheless, there is a difference between *getting in* and *staying in* the covenant of grace. The steadfast love of God endures forever; but like the Ephesians, we can tend to forget our first love and give our hearts to other things (Rev 2:4). Remembering our baptism should lead us to thankfulness but also convince us of the need to renew our covenant with God. This means embracing a commitment to costly discipleship.

Spiritual Amnesia and Covenant Renewal

We have seen that infant baptism was the dominant custom at the time of Wesley. He assumed the generality of Christians had "sinned away" their baptism and broken their covenant with God. In this context, the practice of covenant renewal was an evangelistic call to conversion as well as a recommitment to serious discipleship. Walter Brueggemann has argued that "the church suffers from profound amnesia" about its covenant relationship with God and that "the evangelization of insiders (i.e. most of the whole of the Western church) may be our primary agenda."[2]

Before examining the Wesleyan practice of covenant renewal in some detail, let us look at its origins in Scripture.

Covenant Renewal in the Old Testament

Remembrance was at the heart of Israel's faith and worship. At the annual feast of Passover, they told the story of the Exodus when God had set them free from slavery in Egypt. They were reminded how God gave the law to Moses and entered into a covenant with them, which set them apart as his holy people (Ex 24). They also remembered their propensity to sin and God's patience to forgive. Remembering these events became a way of renewing their covenant relationship with God, who continued to free them from captivity to the powers of this world so they might live for the praise of his glory before the nations.

After the Exodus, Moses led the Israelites through the wilderness so they could learn how to entrust their lives into the hands of God (Deut 8:1-20). They were taught that God would provide for all their needs if they walked in faithful obedience and humble dependence on him. They freely received manna from heaven, water from rocks, protection from snakes, clothes for their backs, and healing for their feet. Moses kept before them a vision of the promised land, where their wandering would come to an end. But he also feared they would forget the lessons of the wilderness by mimicking the surrounding nations and becoming enthralled by their false gods. So, he warned them not to forget the Lord, for breaking the covenant would be the death of them (Deut 4:9-13, 23-24; 6:10-18; 25:17-19). As they prepared to enter the promised land, he wrote the book of the law with instructions for renewing the covenant every seven years (Deut 31:9-13).

Moses was eventually succeeded by Joshua, who led the Israelites to their inheritance. He sought to keep the people faithful amid constant temptations to forget who they were and forsake the Lord. His final act of leadership was to retell the story of Exodus and renew their covenant as the people of God. He told them, "Choose for yourselves this day whom you will serve, whether the gods your ancestors served beyond the Euphrates, or the gods of the Amorites, in whose land you are living" (Josh 24:15). Being presented with this stark choice forced them to confront their idolatry and provided a means for true repentance. But Joshua would not allow them to rush into a decision without understanding the full implications of their commitment. He explained that the Lord is a holy and jealous God, who will have no rival in their hearts and lives. Like Moses before him, Joshua warned that breaking the covenant would be the death of them.

As Moses had predicted, the Israelites settled down, and spiritual amnesia settled in (Deut 31:14-29; Jer 2:2-13). They forgot the lessons of the wilderness, took life into their own hands, and flirted with the local gods. Instead of remembering the devotion of their youth, they chased after worthless things and were likened to an unfaithful bride. When trouble came, they did not ask, "Where is the Lord?" Instead, they traded humble dependence on God for prideful self-sufficiency and started to believe their good fortune was a result of their own ingenuity. They turned away from their first love in order to make a life for themselves, and the spiritual life they once knew began to perish. They had forsaken the Lord, the source of living water, and built "cracked cisterns" that could hold no water.

God was patient with his people and sent prophets to call them back to faithfulness. But only when they were enslaved by the Babylonians and taken into exile did they "look to the rock" from which they were hewn (Is 51:1-3). Eventually, God brought them back to Jerusalem to face the ruins of their former life and to begin a new season of faithfulness. Nehemiah led the rebuilding of the walls, and the people of God worked with all their heart to "bring the stones back to life" (Neh 4:2). After the city was resettled, Ezra opened the book of the law and rediscovered the instructions for covenant renewal (Neh 8; Deut 31:9-13). He gathered all the people together and taught them from the book about life in relationship with God. Finally, they celebrated the long-abandoned festival of "booths" by leaving their houses to live in tents to remember the lessons of the wilderness. After this, the people came together in fasting and prayer, repenting of their old ways, and worshiping again the God of Exodus for this new beginning.

We can draw out three basic lessons from this brief history of covenant renewal in the Old Testament. First, God desires to live in covenant relationship with his people. This is a relationship of mutual love and faithfulness in which God promises to provide for our needs when we commit to his ways. Second, if we take God's blessings for granted, we tend to suffer from memory loss and start living for ourselves. The real problem with spiritual amnesia is that our self-centeredness leads us to break the covenant by mimicking the surrounding culture and becoming enthralled by its false gods. Third, our amnesia can only be cured by a combination of remembrance, repentance, and renewal. Remembering the covenant exposes our self-centered complicity with the world. This opens up the possibility of repentance, and renewal follows repentance by intentionally binding ourselves again to the ways of God and his purposes in the world.

Covenant Renewal in the New Testament

It is possible to see the mission of Jesus in terms of covenant renewal. Just as Israel discovered its identity by crossing the Red Sea, so Jesus passed through the Jordan in baptism and was identified before all the people as the Son of God. Like Israel, he was led through the wilderness to demonstrate the nature of faithful obedience and humble dependence on God. He then formed a community of twelve disciples, symbolizing the twelve tribes of Israel, and renewed the covenant with them on a mountain, just as Moses had done before him. Israel was meant to be a light among the gentiles, so Jesus was sent as light of the world and called his disciples to shine in the darkness. In short, Jesus rebooted the vocation of Israel by gathering a new community of disciples and co-workers in God's mission. This is what it means for us to be the church, the renewed people of God.

Being baptized is a sign of our participation in this unfolding story. In the moment of baptism, we join the movement of Jesus. Passing through the water is our exodus from the world of sin and death and our identification with the people of God. Baptism in the name of the Father means entering into a new covenant relationship with God and sharing his purposes in the world. Baptism in the name of the Son means dying to our old life and entering into a new life of discipleship marked by holy love and obedient faith. And baptism in the name of the Spirit means having the law written on our hearts, so our lives might be transformed into the likeness of Jesus from the inside out.

Nevertheless, the same kind of spiritual amnesia that plagued Israel remains one of the greatest threats to the life of the church (1 Cor 10:1-22; Heb 3:7-19). That is why remembrance is also at the heart of Christian faith and worship. Jesus celebrated the last supper with his disciples at the time of Passover and said, "Do this in remembrance of me" (Lk 22:19). We are baptized only once, but regular participation in the Lord's Supper is a way remembering our baptism and renewing our covenant with God. In the breaking of bread, we remember the death and resurrection of Jesus as an act of atonement through which our sins are forgiven. When we share the cup of the new covenant (1 Cor 11:25), we remember that through this "at-one-ment," he makes a way of entering and renewing our covenant relationship with the Father through the gift of the Spirit. Paul said that by eating and drinking we "proclaim the Lord's death until he comes" (11:26). In other words, sharing in the bread and wine is a renewed commitment to whole-life and lifelong discipleship.[3]

Covenant Renewal in the Wesleyan Tradition

From the sixteenth century, covenantal thinking became a cornerstone of Puritan theology. James Packer summed up Puritan spirituality as the pursuit of a "God-centered life."[4] The Puritans were not merely interested in reforming the structures of the church but in pursuing the goal of spiritual maturity. Real discipleship meant growing in covenant relationship with God by developing an awareness of his presence and providence in all things. They emphasized the disciplines of self-examination and abandonment to the will of God in the unfolding circumstances of daily life. Good stewardship of each person's time, talents, and resources was the basis for practical love of God and neighbor. To this end, they retrieved the biblical idea of covenant renewal and adapted it into a regular spiritual discipline. By the mid-seventeenth century, new converts were encouraged to write a signed and sealed personal covenant with God as a commitment to discipleship.

Approximately one hundred years later, Wesley drew upon this established but neglected practice and made it a distinctive feature of the early Methodist movement.[5] He adapted Richard Alleine's work, *Vindiciae Pietatis: Or a Vindication of Godliness* (1664) into a tract called *Directions for Renewing Our Covenant with God*.[6] Following the example of Moses and Ezra, these directions called for an extended period of catechesis and self-examination to prepare for the act of renewal itself. The early Methodists worked through them in society gatherings for several days and more closely in class and band meetings.

Finally, a "Covenant Service" would be held, in which the whole society was led through a formal liturgy, culminating in a lengthy prayer of commitment and sharing the Lord's Supper. They prayed, "I do here resign my Heart to Thee that made it," promising "to forsake all that is dear to me in this World," and "beseeching thee also to help me against the temptations of Satan." So, "I call heaven and earth to record this day, that I do here solemnly avouch thee for the Lord my God." And, "I do here take Thee the Lord Jehovah, Father, Son, and Holy Ghost, for my portion; and do give up myself, body and soul, for thy Servant; promising and vowing to serve thee in holiness and righteousness, all the days of my life."[7] The language of this prayer deliberately alludes to the marriage covenant, as we bind ourselves to Jesus in bride-like discipleship.[8] The following part of the prayer is worth quoting at length:

> "I do here with all my power accept thee, and take thee for my Head and Husband, for better, for worse, for richer, for poorer, for all times and conditions, to love, honor, and obey thee before all others, and this to the death . . . I do here covenant with thee, to take my lot, as it falls, with thee, and by thy grace assisting, to run all hazards with thee, verily purposing that neither death nor life shall part between thee and me . . . Lord God Omnipotent, Father, Son, and Holy Ghost, Thou art now become my Covenant-Friend, and I through thine infinite grace, am become thy Covenant-Servant. Amen. So be it. And the Covenant which I have made on earth, let it be ratified in heaven."[9]

Covenant renewal became an annual event, held at the start of every new year. This has continued as a more or less permanent feature of British and Irish Methodism, although the tradition is largely forgotten in The United Methodist Church. Over time, however, the rubric has been gradually softened, and the season of preparation reduced to a brief liturgy adapted for a Sunday morning service. The challenging language of entering and renewing a marriage covenant with God is lost altogether. Yet, despite these accommodations to the spiritual tepidity of the contemporary church, the prospect of covenant renewal is still too exacting for many. When the time comes for holding a covenant service, people will stay at home because they cannot face the implications of making such a commitment.

Sadly, our approach to discipleship has been deeply shaped by the individualistic, consumerist, and commitment-phobic habits of contemporary culture. The growing reluctance of people to enter into marriage and the appalling statistic of marriages that quickly end in divorce are indications of our inability to make and keep whole-life and lifelong commitments. Taking the challenge of covenanted discipleship seriously will challenge us to the core.

The truth is, we can only pray the covenant prayer if we are willing to face our spiritual amnesia by remembering God's love for us, repenting of our waywardness, and renewing our commitment to serious discipleship. We can pray this prayer only if we are prepared to unlearn much of what the world has taught us about life, especially where it blinds us to the beauty of scriptural holiness. We can pray this prayer only if we know there is something seductive about worldliness that conspires with our self-centeredness and makes us resistant to following Jesus. And we can pray this prayer only in the presence of a Christian community that will help us see our lives differently, hear his call persuasively, and respond to him more faithfully. It makes no sense for local churches to hold covenant services unless they are committed to making and nurturing disciples who can fulfill the vows they take.

THE COVENANT OF BAPTISM AND DISCIPLESHIP

The only occasion Wesley explicitly described the Christian life in terms of baptism comes in his *Directions* for covenant renewal. He presents them as a form of words "aptly accommodated to all the substantials of our baptismal Covenant."[10] As such, he explains it is for the benefit "not only of young Converts but of the more grown Christians that have not experienced this or the like course."

Wesley pointed out "there is a twofold covenanting with God, In Profession, [and] in Reality: an entering our names, or an engaging our hearts."[11] First, *covenanting in profession* is done by "all that are baptized, who by receiving that Seal of the Covenant are visibly, or in Profession, entered into it." Baptism is "entering our names" in the covenant of grace. In this sense, every Christian is baptized on the profession of faith, whether this is the personal affirmation of adult converts or the corporate inclusion of infants by the church. Either way, this profession goes no further than nominal Christianity until it is followed by a personal commitment to put faith into action.

Second, *covenanting in reality* means "engaging our hearts" by pledging ourselves to the life of discipleship, and this has two aspects. There is a "virtual" commitment, rooted in the decision to give up one's life to God, and this is likened to the state of engagement or betrothal to be married. Then there is a "formal" commitment likened to marriage itself, which is made through "binding ourselves to the Lord by [a] solemn vow or promise to stand to our choice."

This formal commitment can be done in private as a merely inward pledge. But private commitment is much weaker and more susceptible to failure than making an outward commitment in the presence of many witnesses. Wesley urged this visible kind of covenanting with God. Although renewing the covenant was a deeply personal matter, it was to be made face-to-face with others in the Methodist society. The fellowship of classes and bands was necessary for helping one another keep the vows they had made. We will explore this more fully in the next two chapters.

RENEWING OUR COVENANT WITH GOD

Wesley began by urging the reader to remember the seriousness of the present undertaking, "that upon your present choice depends your eternal lot." So, "choose Christ and his ways, and you are blessed for ever; refuse, and you are undone for ever."[12] From the beginning, the people of God have been faced with a choice between life under the reign of God or submission to the deathly powers of this world. Before leaving the wilderness, Moses led Israel through the steps of covenant renewal and confronted them with the need to make an intentional decision: "I have set before you life and death, blessings and curses. Now choose life . . .love the Lord your God, listen to his voice, and hold fast to him. For the Lord is your life" (Deut 30:19-20). Joshua repeated this same choice after Israel entered the promised land. It was repeated by Ezra on their return from exile, by Jesus with his community of disciples, and now by Wesley for the people called Methodists. To help us make the right choice, he guides us along a journey of self-examination in preparation for the prayer of commitment.

Make Your Choice

First, the world has taught us that happiness consists in being self-determined and choosing whatever lifestyle we prefer. We are told that fullness of life comes from having an abundance of opportunities and the freedom to choose which way we will go from one day to the next. In a world like this, it is easy to forget that we are not our own and that true blessedness comes from submission to the purposes of God. But two words from Jesus have the power to awaken us from spiritual amnesia: "Follow me!" This invitation is not a question: "Will you follow me?" Nor is it one more option among others: "You should consider following me." It is a command, which in the very issuing of it denies the possibility of neutrality. Either we will follow Jesus, or we will not!

Consider the story of the rich man (Mk 10:17-22) who knelt before Jesus and asked, "What must I do to inherit eternal life?" Jesus concluded with the command, "Go, sell what you own, and give the money to the poor . . . then come, follow me." The response of the rich man did not reveal a neutral, take-it-or-leave-it attitude. Rather, we are told, "When he heard this, he was shocked and went away grieving because he had many possessions." In that moment, the need to choose exposed a subtle competition for the soul of the rich man. Walking away in grief was not a sign of his freedom; it revealed his bondage to worldliness.

The practice of covenant renewal is deeply challenging because it unmasks our captivity to the illusion of self-determination. Wesley made it clear that if we will not yield our lives to Christ, it is because they are already yielded to the world. There is no neutrality. He said, "Make your choice . . . turn either to the right-hand or to the left . . . Christ with his yoke, his cross and his crown; or the Devil with his wealth, his pleasure and curse."[13] There is no neutral ground upon which we can stand. If we are not consciously yielding our lives to Jesus, we are unconsciously yielding them to this world. The ever-present lure of worldliness has made a claim upon us from birth and has raised us in its sinful ways. Jesus makes his claim upon us through the invitation to discipleship and the promise of new birth into his way of life.

The freedom of a Christian does not lie in a general capacity of choice but in being confronted with a particular kind of choice. The decision we must make is to deny ourselves by following Jesus. We are freed from bondage to worldliness only insofar as we bind ourselves to him and count the cost of discipleship. The more vigorously we bind ourselves to Jesus, the more we are set loose from the world. But the opposite is also true: "If you be unresolved, you are resolved; if you remain undetermined for Christ, you are determined for the Devil."[14]

Covenant renewal presents us with an invitation to unconditional obedience that reveals exactly who, or what, is lord over our lives. That is why it makes no sense to avoid attending a covenant service. Doing so simply declares our lack of faith and our captivity to the world. Yet that is also why we must hold them. Remembering our baptism means knowing there is a competition for our souls and intentionally choosing to resist the world by following Jesus. This is true repentance.

Embark with Christ

Second, the world has taught us that happiness consists in being self-sufficient and remaining in control of our lives. We are told that fullness of life comes from our independence and freedom to keep the future in our own hands. Yielding to the authority of others or being dependent upon them is a sign of weakness rather than strength. In a world like this, it is easy to forget that we are not our own and that true blessedness comes from humble dependence on God. Two more words have power to awaken us from this spiritual amnesia: 'Trust me!' Again, this must be heard neither as a question nor an option but as a command to place our lives into his hands in the face of an unknown future. And again, there is no neutrality. Any unwillingness to submit to the authority of Jesus in complete dependence on him reveals the extent to which we are already captivated by the illusion of self-sufficiency.

Consider how Jesus called his first disciples and the immediacy with which Simon-Peter, Andrew, James, and John dropped their nets (Mt 4:18-22; Mk 1:16-20). Matthew and Levi also wasted no time in walking right out of their tax booths to follow him (Mt 9:9; Mk 2:13-14; Lk 5:27-28). The urgency of his

call and the immediacy of their response set forth a chain reaction in which one follower invited another to "come and see"
(Jn 1:35-51). This may be contrasted with those would-be disciples whose indecision got the better of them (Lk 9:59-62). To the
man whose greatest concern was for securing his inheritance,
Jesus said, "Follow me, and let the dead bury their own dead."[15]
To the man whose greatest concern was old family ties, Jesus
said, "No one who puts a hand to the plow and looks back is fit
for service in the kingdom of God." The cost of discipleship is
making the kingdom of God our greatest concern and following
Jesus, no matter what.

The practice of covenant renewal is deeply challenging
because it exposes our desire for control by unmasking the illusion of self-sufficiency. Wesley invites us to "embark with Christ"
or "adventure yourselves with him."[16] We embark on an "adventure" for which there is no advance preparation but hearing the
gospel and no advance planning but obedient trust. We cannot
negotiate the course of an adventure before we embark upon it,
and Jesus did not negotiate the terms of discipleship with those
he called. Had he done so, it is likely those first disciples would
have stayed home. Christian discipleship is an adventure because
it requires a decision to embark on a lifetime of following without knowing what that commitment will entail. There is nothing
we bring to the relationship except our faithful obedience and
humble dependence. But if you put your trust in Jesus, "he will
bring you home."[17]

Remembering our baptism means accepting that we cannot
know in advance where Jesus will lead us, whom we will have to
embrace, or what pain and suffering we may be called to endure.
We cannot know the depth of our bondage to the world apart from
the temptations to quit along the way. The decision to follow Jesus
must be made every day.

Yield Yourselves to the Lord

Finally, the world has taught us that happiness consists in being self-governing and disposing of our lives the way we see fit. We are told that fullness of life comes from the freedom to do what we want with the things we possess and ensuring that everything we do is for our own benefit. In a world like this, it is easy to forget that we are not our own and that true blessedness comes from surrendering ourselves to God. Two final words of Jesus have power to awaken us from spiritual amnesia: "Deny yourself!" Once again, this must be heard as a command, to yield our lives to his lordship and leading. This is not optional, and there is no neutrality. We belong to God and are called to serve him as good stewards of all that we have and all that we are. Self-denial means giving up the illusion that we are the owners and governors of our lives.[18]

The practice of covenant renewal is deeply challenging because it exposes our captivity to the illusion of self-government and the desire to be masters of our own destiny. The real question is not whether we will be servants, but who will be our master. The Psalmist said to the Lord, "I am yours"; and Jesus in Gethsemane said, "Not my will, but yours be done." The choice is not between serving ourselves or serving the Lord; it is between denying ourselves or being enslaved to the world. If our lives are not yielded up to God through Jesus, we join "those that yield themselves to Sin, and the World," who say in their hearts, "Sin, I am thine; World, I am thine."[19]

Jesus said, "Whoever wants to be my disciple must deny themselves and take up their cross daily and follow me" (Lk 9:23). In light of this, Wesley claimed that self denial is "absolutely, indispensably necessary, either to our becoming or continuing as His disciples." First, "if we do not continually deny ourselves, we do not learn of Him, but of other masters." Second, "if we do not take up our cross daily, we do not come after Him, but after the world, or the prince of the world, or our own fleshly mind."[20] The true disciple "must choose the one or the other; denying God's will, to follow his own; or denying himself, to follow the will of God."[21] Wesley reminds us, "Christ has many services to be done . . . some are suitable to our inclinations and interests, others are contrary to both." Either way, "it will cost us shame and reproach; sailing against the wind, swimming against the tide, steering contrary to the time; parting with our ease, our liberties, and accommodations for the Name of our Lord Jesus."[22]

Just like the first disciples, we must make the decision to follow Jesus without knowing where it might lead because his will for our lives is non-negotiable. Wesley tells us, "Do not think of compounding, or making your own terms with Christ, that will never be allowed you." We must be content that he will "choose your work, and choose your condition; that he should have the command of you, and the disposal of you."[23] The prayerful response that Wesley offers is worth quoting at length:

"I put myself wholly into thy hands: put me to what thou wilt, rank me with whom thou wilt; put me to doing, put me to suffering, let me be employed for thee, or laid aside for thee, or trodden under foot for thee; let me be full, let me be empty, let me have all things, let me have nothing. I freely, and heartily resign all to thy pleasure and disposal."[24]

Remembering our baptism means "closing with Christ as your King and sovereign Lord." Yielding ourselves to the Lord is how we fulfill the baptismal vows of resisting sin, the flesh, and the devil. Wesley said this is "wherein the essence of Christianity lies." When we truly place ourselves under his lordship, "you are Christians indeed, and never till then." He sums up by asserting, "Christ will be the Saviour of none but his Servants . . . Christ will have no Servants but by consent . . . and Christ will accept of no consent but in full . . . he will be all in all, or he will be nothing."[25]

REMEMBERING OUR BAPTISM

Perhaps the lack of vitality in our lives and churches is due to spiritual amnesia that is induced by our propensity toward the self-centered ways of this world. The cure for amnesia is remembrance, and the implication of remembrance is the need to renew our covenant with God. Let us summarize how the regular practice of covenant renewal can provide an authentic approach to remembering our baptism.

- **Initiation into the life of discipleship**. Renewing our covenant with God will not let us settle for a vision of discipleship that is compromised by sin. If we find the demands of whole-hearted surrender to be scandalous, it is most likely because we have already given our hearts to the pursuit of worldly self-interest. If the demands for whole-life devotion seem too great, it is most likely because we have forgotten that God has sacrificed everything to win our hearts and make us his own. A recent form of the covenant prayer opens with the pledge, "I am no longer my own, but yours . . ." and closes with the promise, "You are mine and I am yours." We make and keep this covenant as disciples of Jesus, in the power of his Spirit. The question, "Will we choose to follow him?" Remembering our baptism means honestly facing our temptations to resist and decline this invitation. And renewing our covenant means refusing to let these temptations have the last word in our lives.

- **Dedication to the pursuit of holiness**. After Jesus was baptized, the Spirit descended upon him and the Father's voice declared over him, "You are my Son, whom I love."

Not long after, he told the disciples, "My food is to do the will
of him who sent me and to finish his work" (Jn 4:34). This
relationship of love and obedience took him all the way to
the cross and had the power to overcome death itself. To be a
follower of Jesus means sharing in his life-giving and death-
defeating relationship with the Father through the indwelling power of the Spirit. The question is, "Will we trust our
lives to his hands?" Remembering our baptism means opening ourselves again to the Spirit of adoption that cries out,
"Abba, Father!" And renewing our covenant means living as
though all we say about God is actually true, so that others
might encounter the reality of his love and grace in us.

- **Participation in the mission of God.** "You are mine and
  I am yours." These are not merely words of personal devotion but a prayer of missionary commitment. By claiming
  the promise, "You are mine," we come before God as *ben-
  eficiaries* of his love and grace, so we can be empowered to
  follow Jesus wherever he may lead. By making the pledge, "I
  am yours," we come before God as good *stewards* of his love
  and grace, surrendering ourselves to his service wherever he
  may send us. The question is, "Will we yield ourselves to his
  purposes?" Remembering our baptism means affirming our
  membership of the covenant as *recipients* of God's mission in
  the world. And renewing our covenant means taking up our
  responsibility as *participants* in God's mission to bring others
  into the covenant of his kingdom.

- **Collaboration in disciple-making fellowship.** "Let us
  hold unswervingly to the hope we profess, for he who promised is faithful. And let us consider how we may spur one
  another on toward love and good deeds, not giving up meeting together, as some are in the habit of doing, but encouraging one another—and all the more as you see the Day
  approaching" (Heb 10:23-25). The invitation to renew our

covenant with God must be reckoned with personally, but it cannot be taken up privately. It is only through Christian fellowship that we are empowered to fulfill the promises we have made. The question is, "Will we submit ourselves to meeting for mutual accountability and spiritual guidance?" Remembering our baptism means accepting that we are capable of making an unconditional commitment to follow Jesus only because we are unconditionally dependent on his forgiveness and grace to help us fulfill our promises. But we can walk worthy of that love only as we encourage and exhort one another to live ever more faithfully as his disciples (Heb 10:29, 39).

In the next chapter we will see how renewing our covenant cannot be separated from belonging to a community of disciples on mission with God.

Questions for Group Discussion

1. After reading this chapter, how have your views changed about covenant and discipleship?
2. How does our contemporary culture lead us into the condition of spiritual amnesia or forgetfulness of who and whose we are? What are the dangers of forgetting who and whose we are?
3. What part does the practice of covenant renewal play in the life of your church? Why do you think some Christians might avoid attending a covenant service?
4. What do you find is the most challenging aspect of covenant renewal? Is it making a decision for Christ, following him on the journey of discipleship, or yielding to his lordship in daily life?
5. Which parts of the fourfold pattern for remembering our baptism at the conclusion of this chapter do you find the most challenging? How is the Spirit guiding you?

The Shape of Missional Community

According to the grace given to you, will you remain faithful members of Christ's holy Church and serve as Christ's representatives in the world? Will you who sponsor these candidates support and encourage them in their Christian life? Do you, as Christ's body, the Church, reaffirm both your rejection of sin and your commitment to Christ? Will you nurture one another in the Christian faith and life and include these persons now before you in your care?[1]

Remembering our baptism means being a community of disciples whose orienting concern is to evangelize our neighbors. Do you belong to a community that invites others to embark on the journey of discipleship?

Candidates for baptism make vows to participate in the mission of Jesus to evangelize a lost and broken world. At the same time, the whole church is invited to renew its commitment to discipleship, as a community among whom the newly baptized

Christian can grow in this vocation. The question is, "How do we become such a community?"

"We have been heathens, as you are, for men are not born, but made Christians."[2] Tertullian wrote this in the second century to explain that being a Christian is not an ethnicity. Disciples are made through a process of conversion, no matter where they live or what background they come from. We have also been left with *The Apostolic Tradition of Hippolytus*, which describes how this happened in the first three centuries of the church.[3] True conversion was not merely a change of heart but a transformation of one's whole life, and evangelism was a process that took time. Seekers who responded to the gospel and were ready for a radical change of life were invited to join a group of "catechumens," which literally means "those who hear" the teaching of Jesus. This began a journey of training in the life of discipleship that culminated in the decision to be baptized.

Wesley observed a similarity between the Methodist society and the early church catechumenate. In both cases, when the preachers found those who "were so convinced of the truth, as to forsake sin and seek the gospel salvation, they immediately joined them together, took an account of their names, advised them to watch over each other, and met these *kathcoumenoi*, 'catechumens' . . . apart from the great congregation, that they might instruct, rebuke, exhort, and pray with them, and for them, according to their several necessities."[4]

In this chapter, we will explore Wesley's insight by making a comparison between the process of evangelism in the early church and the practices of disciple making in the early Methodist movement. Remembering our baptism will challenge us to consider what it means for the contemporary church to be a missional community that has disciple making as its orienting concern.

EVANGELISM IN THE EARLY CHURCH

We will begin by examining how the cultural context of the early church shaped its approach to evangelism and mission and its life together as a missional community.[5]

The Context of Mission

Discipleship in the early church was tough. First, the sporadic persecution of Christians continued from the time of Emperor Nero until the Edict of Milan (313 CE) that granted them religious freedom. Persecution turned into systemic hostility in the third century when Emperor Decius issued an edict requiring every citizen to demonstrate loyalty to the empire by making sacrifices to the Roman gods. Christians were forbidden to worship false gods or pledge allegiance to any lord other than Jesus. So they were forced to make a choice between submission to the powers of this world or resisting them and living under the threat of death. Some renounced their faith and others went into hiding to save their lives. Still others counted the full cost of discipleship and laid down their lives for Jesus and his kingdom. From the beginning of the church, martyrdom has been a powerful form of witness. Refusing to be silenced, Tertullian himself said, "Do your worst . . . it is all to no purpose; you do but attract the world and make it fall the more in love with our religion; the more you mow us down, the thicker we rise; the Christian blood you spill is like the seed you sow, it springs from the earth again, and fructifies the more."[6]

Second, the powers of evil were not merely external and coercive but internal and seductive. In addition to emperor worship and polytheism, Roman culture was fascinated by occult religion and the magic arts. The early church knew that sin was not simply a matter of behaving badly but a propensity of the selfish heart to become enslaved by spiritual forces of evil. Paul characterized these marks of pagan life as "works of the flesh," which are "sexual immorality, impurity, and debauchery; idolatry and witchcraft; hatred, discord, jealousy, fits of rage, selfish ambition, dissensions, factions, and envy; drunkenness, orgies, and the like." Whether they were being forcibly persecuted or not, the Christians were in a spiritual war zone. Only the power of the Spirit could set them free from these powers of sin and death. As Paul urges, "Walk by the Spirit, and you will not gratify the desires of the flesh" (Gal 5:16-21).

The Nature of Conversion

In the midst of this dominant culture, the lives of Christians were visibly different. They were committed to scriptural holiness in everyday life, whether at home, among their neighbors, or in the workplace. Aristides wrote one of the earliest "apologies" of the church (around 125 CE), urging the emperor to consider how the lives of Christians outshone the pagan citizens.[7] He drew attention to their sexual discipline, truthfulness, financial reliability, care toward the needy, and love for all their neighbors, whether friends, strangers, or enemies. The central concern of the church was to prepare, train, and support this living witness to the gospel.

One of the first training manuals in the early church, known as *The Didache*, defined true discipleship as a daily choice between the way of Jesus and the way of the world.[8] These two ways recall the biblical mandate to choose between a life-giving covenant with God or slavery to the powers of sin and death. The real challenge, however, was not learning how they should live but actually putting their faith into practice no matter what the cost. This training demanded a form of apprenticeship that could be supplied only by a community of disciples who lived alongside one another as examples, guides, and mentors. The early church labored to embody a way of life that was worthy of imitation.

In around 150 CE, Justin Martyr argued that life shaped by Roman culture was positively addictive and true freedom could be found only among the Christians. Conversion was not merely about choosing the way of Jesus but unlearning the ways of the world and renouncing the demonic powers that lay behind them. In a world where sexuality was marred by the demon of fornication, Christians were set free to live faithfully in stable marriages. Where spiritual life was trapped by the demon of magical arts, Christians were set free for wholehearted devotion to God. Where commerce was impaired by the demon of competitive self-interest, Christians were set free to share all they had with others. Where relationships were poisoned by the demons of violence and xenophobia, Christians were set free to love their neighbors and even their enemies. True conversion was the transformation of lives from darkness to light, from the kingdom of this world to the kingdom of God (Rev 11:15). As Tertullian argued, the beauty of their lives was not because they were born that way, but because they had been reborn as children of God and had inherited a whole other set of family traits.

The Spread of the Gospel

How did the gospel message spread so rapidly among people so deeply ingrained in the Roman culture when they viewed Christianity as an odious and superstitious cult? Alan Kreider argues that, "Christianity grew by attraction."[9] Unbelievers were attracted to the gospel by the growing reputation of the church and through personal encounters with Christians in everyday settings.

They were known for serving the needs of those who lived without hope in the world, irrespective of their social or religious standing. They visited the sick and prisoners, the poor and hungry, the widows and orphans, and all those without means to take care of themselves. They collected money, as well as stocks of food and clothing, to distribute according to need, whether they were inside or outside the church. And they were known for sexual purity, faithfulness in marriage, and hospitality in their homes. The church gave a visible confidence to women, a new sense of belonging to servants, and a greater intimacy between parents and children. All were equally wanted and valued, brothers and sisters in Christ, and active members of his kingdom. Tertullian noted that outsiders would say, "Look ye . . . how these Christians seem to love each other."[10]

They stood out by a commitment to nonviolence and the sanctity of life. Christian families adopted female babies left on rubbish dumps to die and saved young children abandoned as worthless on city streets. They did not practice abortion and rescued many women who had been rendered childless by it. They refused to condone violence masquerading as entertainment by refusing to watch the gladiatorial games and other blood sports.

Moreover, the early Christians were conspicuous for the appearance of supernatural power in their lives. They were able to "live the gospel" without fear, even in the midst of persecution. Unbelievers sensed in this freedom a power that might free them from bondage to the addictions they felt in their own hearts. Rumors of exorcism and life-changing prayer were a major attraction to a people longing for real freedom and hope for the future.

In many ways, the social context of the West today has much more in common with the pagan culture surrounding the early church than the Christendom of Wesley's eighteenth century. But insofar as early Methodism shared the same impulses as the early church, there is real insight to be gained for the task of making disciples in our emerging post-Christendom situation.

A Pattern for Making Disciples

Making disciples in the early church was not just one activity among many, but the organizing center of its life and worship. Consistent with the Great Commission, the church's process of making disciples centered on the practice of baptism. The story of Philip and the Ethiopian eunuch illustrates the connection between evangelism, baptism, and disciple making in the early church (Acts 8:26-50).[11] There was a seeker, the Ethiopian, whose heart was already open to the Lord, but he lacked a spiritual guide. There was an obedient disciple, Philip, who was walking closely with the Lord and was sent by the Spirit to walk alongside the seeker. There was teaching, as Philip explained the gospel to the Ethiopian eunuch in a journey of deep conversation and struggle to understand the truth. There was a decision made by the Ethiopian, prompted by the sight of water, which elicited a discussion about the meaning of baptism. There was a baptism, in which both men passed through the water together and rose up as Spirit-filled brothers in Christ. Finally, there was discipleship, as the Spirit moved Philip on in mission and set the Ethiopian eunuch on his way with a new song in his mouth.

Paradoxically, this story has been used as an argument for baptizing people without delay as well as adopting a more protracted approach to the preparation of candidates for baptism. In the early church, these two methods were complementary but adapted to the nature of the convert. For example, Jews and proselytes could be baptized immediately because their lives had already been shaped by kingdom values in a community of faith. The Ethiopian eunuch and most other examples from Scripture would fall into this category. For everyone else, however, conversion required a detoxification from the ways of worldliness, which would take time because the addictions ran deep. The *Apostolic Tradition* outlines a process of making such disciples with four distinct stages.

Evangelizing

Unlike many contemporary approaches to church growth, these missional communities did not advance through cultural accessibility but through spiritual attraction. It was not the inner life of the church that attracted seekers because their gatherings were generally closed to outsiders, but the outer life and witness of Christians in the world. Rodney Stark has argued that this attractive life was formed within the Christian community and flowed out in ever increasing circles of witness, from the home into the workplace and through all their existing networks of relationship.[12] The everyday lives of Christians were signs that pointed back to the communities that empowered them and created among outsiders a desire to find out more.

Christians took their inquiring friends to meet the church leaders, who examined them to discern whether they were ready to change their lives and give up any behavior that ran counter to the gospel. Some would be expected to leave their occupations altogether; for example, actors celebrating false gods, prostitutes steeped in sexual immorality, and gladiators who made sport of murdering others.[13] Put simply, the first step in the journey of discipleship was true repentance, and those who proved to be teachable were admitted to the catechumenate. The missional logic of this process is inescapable. If the gospel was spread through the radically different lifestyle of church members, then compromise would carry the seeds of its own destruction. From the moment of welcome, seekers became disciples of Jesus, representatives of the community, and witnesses in the world.

Discipling

Those who brought their inquiring friends into the community also journeyed alongside them as sponsors, examples, and guides.

The catechumens were "hearers" of the word. In Scripture, the word "hear" (Hebrew, *shema*) encompasses a range of meaning from merely listening to "taking heed," or simply doing what is asked of us. James urges, "Do not merely listen to the word, and so deceive yourselves. Do what it says" (Jam 1:22; also Ex 24:7). We have truly heard, only when the teaching of Jesus changes our heart and transforms our lives. The catechumens were trained by participation in a countercultural body of people who set them an example of holy living and held them accountable for practicing what they professed. But the catechumens were also separated from the rest of the community for training more suited to the discipling of seekers. Robert Webber suggests this "catechesis" had three basic ingredients.[14]

First, they were trained in spiritual warfare. The biblical word "hear" also carries the meaning of "pledging allegiance." Like soldiers, the catechumens learned how to exchange their unthinking submission to worldliness for conscious obedience to the lordship of Jesus. Through a kind of apprenticeship to their catechists, a small group of catechumens learned how to renounce their old ways in the world and commit to the way of discipleship. This retraining of heart and life was accomplished by learning the disciplines of fasting, prayer, giving, and costly service, as weapons against the spiritual powers of worldliness. John Chrysostom also described the catechumenate as a "wrestling school" that trained the catechumens to struggle against sinful temptations and persevere through cycles of breakthrough and backsliding (Gen 32:22-32).

A second theme is discipleship as a journey. The catechumens were like the Israelites making an exodus from Egypt, forming a new identity among the people of God, and learning the lessons of the wilderness. They were in a liminal state, having crossed the Red Sea and waiting to cross the Jordan to enter the promised land as baptized members of the kingdom.

Finally, the church is likened to a mother. The catechumenate is the womb of the church, and the catechumens are in a period of gestation. Once formed, they were ready to pass through the amniotic waters of baptism as newborn members of the family.

The time spent as a catechumen would be as long as needed for each person to evidence the marks of true conversion. This included a change of mind through the acquisition of sound doctrine and a change of heart through the development of godly habits. Both were evidenced in a life dedicated to caring for the poor, the widows, and the sick, as well as other works of mercy. When catechumens made the decision to be baptized, their friends vouched for them before the leaders. Successful candidates were then enrolled by name into a covenant with God and the community. Then they entered an intensive period of pre-baptismal training.

Equipping

At this stage, the candidates for baptism were separated again, not merely as hearers of "the word," but hearers of "the gospel." Kreider interprets this to mean the good news of new birth and the privilege of living as the children of God.[15] They meditated on the Creed, learning devotion to the triune God and his saving purposes in the world. They also meditated on the Lord's Prayer, learning how to develop a covenant relationship with God in daily life. He is "Our Father," and our delight is to do his will so the kingdom of heaven may come on earth. These practices were also taken up as weapons of spiritual warfare, along with a season of fasting and prayer in preparation for baptism. They received frequent prayers of exorcism to cast out the powers of sin, the flesh, and the devil.

Finally, they gathered at a source of "living water," like the sea or a river. The bishop would mark them with the sign of the cross and then breathe on their faces to prepare them for being filled with the Spirit. Then they stripped naked and entered the water.

After a final act of renunciation, they were immersed three times in the triune name of God. Once they came out of the water, they were dressed in fresh white garments and anointed with oil for the gift and seal of the Spirit. Then the community welcomed them by sharing "the kiss of peace," and they participated in their first Communion service.

Passing through the water of baptism was a sign of new birth, putting off the old life of worldliness and putting on the new life of discipleship. It was also a sign of dying and rising with Jesus, signifying a readiness to participate in his sufferings as well as his victory over evil. Joining this community meant counting the cost of persecution, a loss of reputation, and even estrangement from the friends and family of their previous life.

Nurturing

The final stage was a period of post-baptismal training aimed at helping the newly born Christians to grow in faith and encouraging them to remain faithful in spite of the challenges that lay ahead. For Clement of Alexandria (150–215), the memory of baptism shaped the whole life of discipleship. He said, "Baptism must so permeate the Christian life that the baptized are not to depart from the image" even while they sleep.[16] But it is the role of the Spirit that rises to prominence in the ongoing nurture of disciples. Cyprian (200–258) explained that they had been born again by the agency of the Spirit, and John Chrysostom (349–407) reminded them that discipleship is only maintained through the continuous leading of the Spirit in daily life.

Drawing on writings from the first part of the fourth century, Raniero Cantalamessa argues there was a season when the early church experienced "an inebriation of the Holy Spirit."[17] Cyril of Jerusalem (313–386) taught catechumens to expect a "sober intoxication" of the Spirit that "purifies of sin, renews the heart in

fervour and enlightens the mind by a special knowledge of God."
In reference to the Lord's Supper, Ambrose of Milan (339–397)
explained that drinking wine not only brings forgiveness of sin but
a spiritual intoxication keeps one "rooted in Christ" and producing
fruit.[18] Seeking the fullness of the Spirit was vital for developing
their gifts as full members of the body and sharing the church's
mission in the world.

METHODIST SOCIETY AS MISSIONAL COMMUNITY

In *A Plain Account of the People Called Methodists*, Wesley outlined
what he called "the whole economy" of the early Methodist movement. He observed that in every new development there was
"something in Christian antiquity likewise, very nearly parallel
thereto."[19] I will now draw out some of those parallels.

Societies

The first Methodist society arose from preaching the gospel to
nominal Christians around London. The initial enthusiasm of
those who responded was lost, however, because they had no
means of pursuing the life of discipleship. So, Wesley gathered
them together for instruction and advice. He defined this society
as a community of disciples who "united themselves in order to
pray together, to receive the word of exhortation, and to watch
over one another in love, that they might help each other to work
out their salvation."[20]

The "one only condition" for entering a society was "a desire
to flee from the wrath to come and be saved from their sins." This
recalls the words of John the Baptist who rebuked the crowds that
came looking for cheap grace and told them to produce fruit in
keeping with true repentance (Jn 3:7-17). The rich must share with
the needy, tax collectors must stop robbing the poor, and soldiers

must stop extorting money from the vulnerable. The message of repentance paved the way for hearing the good news about Jesus and the promise of baptism in the Spirit. This was the main agenda of both the early church and early Methodism.

The Methodist movement was catalyzed by "preaching abroad," which meant proclaiming the gospel outside the confines of a church building wherever they could get a hearing. The goal of such evangelistic preaching was not immediate conversion but spiritual awakening, and those who responded were incorporated into a society. In fellowship with others, they were committed to the *General Rules* of doing no harm and doing all the good one can by attending to works of piety and mercy.[21] These fruits of repentance were the means for pursuing the gift of saving faith and the life of discipleship.[22]

For Wesley, salvation was not merely being saved from the guilt of sin or even from the power of sin, but freedom from all the habits of worldliness that take root in the heart. The goal of evangelism was to initiate seekers into a community of discipleship where sinful habits could be gradually rooted out and godly habits cultivated in their place. This was a gradual process of transformation that aimed at "salvation to the uttermost," in which hearts are entirely ruled by the love of God and neighbor.

In comparing the early church with early Methodism, there is a difficulty when it comes to defining the meaning of "conversion." From the pre-Christendom perspective of the early church, conversion was a holistic process of turning away from pagan lifestyles to embrace the new life of Christian discipleship. Within the Christendom context of early Methodism, however, conversion emphasized the inbreaking experience of justifying and sanctifying grace that turned nominal Christians into real disciples. In this sense, conversion was not a process but an instantaneous moment within a more gradual process of salvation. I suggest that making disciples in our post-Christendom context will mean paying attention to both senses of conversion. We live in a society where the values of scriptural holiness are scorned at best and unknown at worst. So, evangelism will mean inviting people to a whole new way of life that only the revolutionary power of the Spirit can accomplish.

Classes

As the Methodist societies grew in size, it became increasingly difficult for members to watch over one another, and some inevitably gave in to the temptations of the world. Wesley identified three problems with continuing to embrace unrepentant members of the community. First, sin is infectious and others can be led astray. Second, it takes only one person to ruin the reputation of a whole society. Third, because of this, a stumbling block is put in the way of outsiders responding to the truth of the gospel. Failure to deal with sinfulness was a missional issue, because it impeded the whole process of making disciples from beginning to end. The development of "classes" provided a solution to this problem.[23]

Each society was divided up into small groups of about twelve people who met every week for spiritual conversation guided by the *General Rules*. A class meeting would include people at all stages in the journey of discipleship, from seekers to mature believers.[24] As with the catechumenate, members would bring their seeking friends to the meeting. Class leaders would speak first by giving an account of their walk with God over the previous week along with the accompanying state of their souls. The leader then addressed each member in turn and asked a variety of probing questions to draw out their personal experience. This process enabled the comfort and exhortation of genuine seekers, the detection and reproof of insincerity, as well as the exclusion of disruptive and unrepentant sinners. Wesley summed up, "It can scarce be conceived what advantages have been reaped from this little prudential regulation

. . . As they had daily a more intimate acquaintance with, so they had a more endeared affection for, each other. And speaking the truth in love, they grew up into Him in all things, who is the Head, even Christ."[25]

Classes became the basic unit of membership in the Methodist society. Wesley and his assistant preachers developed the practice of quarterly examination for every member. Class leaders would vouch for those who continued to uphold the discipline, and those who did were given a "society ticket."[26] These tickets were named, dated, and reissued every quarter as a means of regulating admission to society meetings. Only after exercising much patience would tickets be withheld and members excluded from the community. Those seeking to join the community were incorporated into a class meeting on a trial basis and admitted to the society only at the next quarterly examination.[27]

The class meeting bears a close comparison with the pre-baptismal catechesis of the early church.[28] In both, the goal was initiating seekers into the way of discipleship and bringing their lives into line with the teaching of Scripture. The role of a class leader was similar to that of catechist, examining the conduct of each member and training by precept and example. By "doing no harm," they learned how to renounce evil of every kind and go the way of repentance. By "doing good," they learned how to love their neighbor through works of mercy.[29] By "attending upon all the ordinances of God," they learned how to stay connected with God's love and grace in the works of piety, on which everything else depended. From the outset, the process of evangelism encouraged people to "live the gospel" in word and deed as a witness to the world.

Finally, the class meeting also mirrored the basic images of the catechumenate. As a journey, seekers left behind their old life in the world to pursue the new life of discipleship. As a wrestling school, members helped one another to resist temptation and hold onto the promises of the gospel. And as the womb of Methodist society, seekers grew in grace and waited for the gift of new birth. The class leader was a guide, a coach, and a midwife. Like the patient process of catechesis in the early church, it could take up to two years of gestation in a class meeting before seekers experienced the moment of evangelical conversion.

Bands

Those who found justifying faith and new birth were put into separate small groups called "bands."[30] Wesley was first introduced to bands among the Moravians, and the name "band" was derived from the German word *bundt,* meaning union or fellowship. If class meetings can be likened to the pre-baptismal catechumenate, the band meeting bears comparison with the post-baptismal nurturing of converts. The meeting itself proceeded in a similar manner to the classes, but provided a means of "closer union" through which the innermost life of the soul could be shared openly. To maximize this intimacy, bands were limited to between four and seven members, each grouped according to gender and age. They also had their own set of penetrating questions for mutual self-examination.[31]

Bands met weekly, focusing on the biblical instruction to "confess your sins to each other and pray for each other so that you may be healed" (Jam 5:16). Confession was not an exercise in guilt management, and the purpose was not merely to seek assurance from God or the sympathy of others. Rather, the goal of confession was healing, which meant being saved from the deeply rooted sin that kept their lives in a state of brokenness. Against accusations of popery, Wesley argued their practice was "the confession of several persons conjointly, not to a Priest, but to each other."[32] Logically speaking, confessing to "one another" cannot be accomplished by private repentance or a one-on-one confessional. Rather, one-anothering requires the shared life of three or more persons.

The spiritual dynamic of the band meeting was characterized by two main features, each with parallels in the early church. First, it was a community of prayer engaged in spiritual warfare. Conversion brought people into a new relationship with God, forgiven of their sins and filled with the Spirit. But this was just the start of a lifelong working relationship with the Spirit to renew hearts and lives in the likeness of Jesus. Wesley explained: "For the war was not over, as they had supposed; but they had still to wrestle both with flesh and blood, and with principalities and powers" that still enslaved their lives.[33] The band meeting was advanced training in the wrestling school of discipleship.

Wesley observed,

"Great and many are the advantages which have ever since flowed from this closer union of the believers with each other. They prayed for one another, that they might be healed of the faults they had confessed; and it was so. The chains were broken, the bands were burst in sunder, and sin had no more dominion over them. Many were delivered from the temptations out of which, till then, they found no way to escape. They were built up in our most holy faith. They rejoiced in the Lord more abundantly. They were strengthened in love and more effectually provoked to abound in every good work."[34]

The second key feature of the band meeting, in parallel with the early church, was the pursuit of holy love. Freedom from the power of sin is freedom for growth in grace. They prayed together for the healing power of the Spirit to overcome their habits of worldliness by implanting the fruit of holiness. To this end, Wesley further diversified these groups to include "penitential bands" for disciples who had momentarily lost sight of God and "select bands" for those desiring to "press after perfection." The select companies were to provide a "pattern of love, of holiness, and of all good works," imitable by members of the whole society.[35] It was often in the bands that class leaders and preachers were raised up.

Grace Murray (1718–1803) traveled frequently with John Wesley as a "fellow-labourer in the gospel," and she was instrumental in the earliest organization of classes and bands among women in the expanding movement. She described how "people were divided into bands, or small select societies; women by themselves, and the men in like manner. I had a full hundred in classes, whom I met in two separate meetings and a band for each day of the week. I likewise visited the sick and backsliders, which was my pleasant meat. The work of God was my delight, and when I was not employed in it I seemed out of my element . . . And oh, what pouring out of the Spirit have I seen in those times!"[36]

Mission

The last third of the *Plain Account* is devoted to describing the missional outreach of the Methodist movement. As in the early church, the process of making disciples was also spiritual formation for mission. Visiting the sick was a discipline expected of everyone and was a ministry often taken up by courageous women.[37] For example, Wesley urged Miss March to "put off the gentlewoman" and go to the uneducated poor: "Creep in among them in spite of dirt and a hundred disgusting circumstances."[38]

Class leaders were also responsible for raising up members with the role of "visitor," set apart to serve the whole society. The responsibility of a visitor was "to inquire into the state of their souls, and to advise them." As well as identifying their bodily needs, the visitor was to "do anything for them, which he (or she) can do."[39] This was a risky ministry for two reasons. First, calling on the sick meant the possibility of catching their diseases. For example, Sarah Peters contracted "a malignant fever" while visiting Newgate Prison in London and died after a few weeks of suffering. Second, when visiting needy households, visitors would share their faith or leave a tract with people, often to be met with abuse and frequent disappointment.[40]

It is also worth noting the development of the "poor house" for the care of aged widows, the blind, and poor children. In both cases, Wesley observed they had inadvertently copied a practice of the early church and boasted, in the manner of Tertullian, "I can now say to all the world, Come and see how these Christians love one another."[41] All these works of mercy were means of grace by which people would grow in discipleship while spreading the gospel.

REMEMBERING OUR BAPTISM

The early church adapted its life to the business of making disciples in a pagan culture that was generally hostile to the Christian faith. The early Methodists organized their life around making disciples in a Christendom culture tinged with kingdom values and a church full of nominal Christians. Ironically, we now live in a post-Christendom situation, in which the mission field looks more like that of the early church, while contemporary Methodism looks more like the spiritually tepid church it originally sought to renew. Put differently, we live in a culture that needs something more like pre-Christendom mission, but we have a church that is stuck in Christendom modes of discipleship. To put it bluntly, churches everywhere are dying because they are full of nominal Christians with leaders who have little expectation of radical discipleship among their members. Let me suggest how reflecting on the early church shapes the practice of remembering our baptism.

- **Initiation into the life of discipleship.** In our post-Christendom society, discipleship must be viewed as a way of holiness that sets us apart from the prevailing culture and will set us against it at crucial points. Pursuing this way of holiness will have to start with the re-evangelization of the church itself as we look for two kinds of conversion. First, there must be authentic repentance, evidenced in real changes of lifestyle to bring us into conformity with the teaching of Jesus. Second, we need to pursue the new birth and baptism in the Spirit to empower authentic transformation from the inside out. The practice of covenant renewal can be a means for committing to this journey of discipleship, and participation in the disciplines associated with the class meeting can be a way of pursuing it. Are we ready to journey on and share that journey with others?

- **Dedication to the pursuit of holiness**. The church grows from the contagious witness of disciples who are made strangely attractive by the gospel. Settling for nominal Christianity will inevitably lead to a failure of evangelism and mission. But the pursuit of radical discipleship comes at a cost to the individual and the church. Evangelism can no longer aim at getting people to make an easy decision for Jesus that allows them to settle for worldly lives propped up by cheap grace. The cost to seekers will be a radical choice for holy living that will turn daily life into a spiritual war zone and that often leaves us swimming against the tide of popular culture. This will be impossible without participation in the disciplines associated with the band meeting. Are we ready to make that choice and submit to these disciplines?

- **Participation in the mission of God**. Making disciples in the early church has reminded us that the baptism of adult converts is the norm and expectation of truly missional communities. In a post-Christendom society, one sign of failure in mission is the absence of believer's baptism in the church. If our communities are to become missional by nature, they will need to organize structures of discipleship around the need for baptizing and nurturing converts. As we have seen, the class meeting can serve to evangelize the baptized members of church and function as a pre-baptismal catechumenate for the initiation of new Christians. Either way, those who experience the new birth should be incorporated into something like band meetings as the primary mark of a baptized disciple. Are we ready to invest our resources and leadership in developing these small groups as a central strategy for making disciples?

- **Collaboration in disciple-making fellowship**. Both the early church and the early Methodist movement call the church to become a community that will not compromise with nominalism or settle for lukewarm discipleship. The cost to the church will be a radical choice to develop a culture of spiritual formation and discipline against the trends of individualism, such as privatized and consumer-driven spirituality. But we will need a wholesome vision of discipleship to carry such an agenda forward. The heart of this will be embracing small-group fellowship as a means of grace. It will mean understanding how mutual accountability and spiritual guidance can help us connect more deeply with the presence and leading of the Spirit in daily life. And it will mean discovering the grace of spiritual friends who are close enough to both comfort and rebuke us on the journey of discipleship. Are we ready to put our trust in the purposes of God by entrusting our lives to the discipline of Christian fellowship?

In the next chapter, we will take a closer look at the inner dynamics of class and band meetings and how they served as contexts of spiritual formation for discipleship and mission.

QUESTIONS FOR GROUP DISCUSSION

1. After reading this chapter, how have your views changed about the nature of church and its part in the mission of God?

2. Does your church have any expectations that members will grow in holiness? How does the quality of our lives make the gospel both attractive and credible to unbelievers? Or, in the words of Wesley, how might the lives of Christians be a stumbling block to the spread of the gospel?

3. In what ways does your church help seekers explore the life of discipleship and bring them to the point of conversion and baptism? How could this be improved?

4. Why should making disciples be the central business of a missional community? What would it take for your church to become such a community?

5. Which parts of the fourfold pattern for remembering our baptism at the conclusion of this chapter do you find the most challenging? How is the Spirit guiding you?

CHAPTER 7

The Discipline of
Christian Fellowship

Do you renounce the spiritual forces of wickedness, reject the evil powers of this world, and repent of your sin? Do you accept the freedom and power that God gives you to resist evil, injustice and oppression in whatever forms they present themselves? Do you confess Jesus Christ as Savior, put your whole trust in his grace, and promise to serve him as your Lord, in union with the church?[1]

Remembering our baptism means recognizing that discipleship is a spiritual struggle against the powers of sin and worldliness. Are you in the kind of fellowship that can help you stand firm and press on?

In baptism, we make vows to reject the evil powers of this world and to live as faithful citizens in the kingdom of God. At the same time, the whole church renews its commitment to help the newly baptized keep their promises.

Baptism is a sacrament of the church. The term *sacrament* is derived from the Latin word *sacramentum,* meaning an oath, vow, or sacred bond. It was used to describe the annual pledge of allegiance made by Roman soldiers to serve the emperor and lay down their lives for him in battle. In the early church, Tertullian argued that baptism was the only pledge of allegiance that Christians should make, committing to serve Jesus as Lord and advance his kingdom on earth.[2] From this perspective, the church may be likened to a "boot camp" for the training of "spiritual warriors." Militaristic images of discipleship tend to be scorned these days, and for some good reasons. But we must not throw the baby out with the baptismal water!

Through baptism, we are plunged into a state of warfare, not against flesh and blood but against the demonic powers of this dark world and the spiritual forces of evil in the heavenly realms (Eph 6:10-12). It is in the context of spiritual struggle and the temptation to quit that Paul urged Timothy to remember his baptism. He said, "Fight the good fight of the faith. Take hold of the eternal life to which you were called when you made your good confession in the presence of many witnesses" (1 Tim 6:12). Susanna Wesley also understood this and drew upon the work of a Theatine monk called Lorenzo Scupoli to help train her children as "spiritual warriors." In his work, *The Spiritual Combat* (1589), Scupoli described the Christian life as a battle for the soul in which there is no peace treaty to be made and no neutral ground on which to stand. His repeated reminder is, "Fight or die."[3]

In this chapter, we will explore how the early Methodists were armed for battle through the discipline of Christian fellowship. Remembering our baptism will challenge us to reflect on whether we are fulfilling our baptismal vows to fight the good fight as disciples and disciple-making communities.

THE NATURE OF OUR SPIRITUAL COMBAT

Central to the great narrative of Scripture is a cosmic battle between good and evil.[4] This battle is waged in heaven but worked out on earth. The evil powers of this world are at work in every human heart and through every human institution. For persecuted Christians around the world, these powers are visible, coercive, and deadly. The rest of us remember these brothers and sisters in our prayers and give thanks for our freedom. Yet the church is growing in places of persecution, while our churches wither and die. The early Methodist movement also grew through persecution and suffering, but they knew the real enemy lay within.[5] Perhaps we are not as free as we thought.

The Powers of This World

In our affluent, post-Christendom culture, the spiritual forces of wickedness are mostly invisible and subtle, but no less deadly. Let's name them. The spiritual force of "individualism" tempts us to live as though life is better if we just look after ourselves, even at the expense of others. The spiritual force of "consumerism" tempts us to live as though we depended on the accumulation of goods and services. The spiritual force of "technicism" tempts us to live as though we will be saved by scientific know-how and find happiness in our gadgets. The spiritual force of "careerism" tempts us to live as though we are defined by our work and find happiness through the pursuit of wealth. I could go on. These cultural forces overcome us by stealth, appealing to the self-centered tendencies within our hearts. Consciously or unconsciously, we yield to their influence over us, believing we are in control but unwittingly surrendering our souls to their deathly grip.

The real question is not whether we are in a battle, but what we are fighting for and who is training us for combat. For both Scupoli and Wesley, the prize of our discipleship is perfection in love. Wesley claimed that the people called Methodists were raised up by God to spread the good news of scriptural holiness and that the doctrine of "Christian perfection" was the great treasure they had to share. Thankfully, he left us with a tract called *The Character of a Methodist* to explain what he meant by perfection.[6] His purpose was to captivate our imaginations with a vision for the fullness of life in Christ "and mostly in the very words of Scripture." Only when we catch sight of the prize will we see the need to fight, and only when we are aware of the battle will we see the need for disciplined Christian fellowship.

The Pursuit of Holiness

Over the years, we have done much to make the idea of "holiness" appear either unattractive or unattainable. Think of monks, saints, and other spiritual elites who have had little to do with everyday life and set impossible examples to follow. Think of "holier-than-thou" people who lead strict moral lives while censuring everyone around them, but often turn out to be hypocrites. Or think of those legalistic types who measure spirituality by conformity to a list of do's and don'ts, while simultaneously removing every drop of enjoyment from life. The idea of "perfection" doesn't do much for us either. We might think of it in absolute moral terms as something reserved for the angels, or as possible for God alone. Alternatively, our technical culture has predisposed us to think of perfection in terms of flawless performance. Both divine perfection and technical perfection are quite beyond human attainment. Far from inspiring a life of virtue and excellence, such expectations of perfection are more likely to engender disillusionment, despondency, and despair.

Wesley himself disavowed such "perfectionism." He said it was "the grand device of Satan" to turn the pursuit of holiness into life-sapping legalism, especially if it discourages us from living up to what we have already attained.[7] As we have already seen, the simple aim of Wesley's teaching was to captivate our imaginations with a scripturally rooted vision of human beings made fully alive in God, as Jesus-shaped and Spirit-filled disciples. So, an underlying theme of *The Character of a Methodist* is that any reader would find only "the common fundamental principles of Christianity." Wesley argued that the Methodists had no uncommon doctrine or discipline to set them apart from other real Christians in any denomination who take the word of God as their rule of faith. The truth is, we are not baptized in the name of "Methodism" or as Presbyterians, Baptists, or Anglicans. We are baptized in the name of our triune God, and the fellowship of the church is organized to help us become more fully devoted followers of Jesus.

The Character of Real Christianity

Drawing on the Great Commandment, Wesley defined his vision for discipleship as the perfect love of God and neighbor. A real Christian is one who has "the love of God shed abroad in his heart by the Holy Ghost given unto him," and who "loves the Lord his God with all his heart, and with all his soul, and with all his mind, and with all his strength." In short, "God is the joy of his heart, and the desire of his soul."[8] The life of God in the soul of human beings is central to every true expression of discipleship and the church. The value of all our doctrine and discipline lies in perfecting this relationship with God and the way of life that flows from it. Wesley developed the two aspects of the Great Commandment to outline this relationship in the following ways.

First, a real Christian is one who "exercises his love to God by praying without ceasing, rejoicing evermore, and in everything giving thanks."[9] It means having our hearts ever lifted up to God, filled by a love that casts out all fear, and content to trust our whole lives into his hands with the sure hope that he works all things together for our good.[10] This covenant of love is embodied in joyful obedience by offering up our whole lives in service to God. With purity of heart, we are to renounce the desires of this world; and with singularity of intention, we look only to fulfill his purposes in all things.[11]

Second, this love of God is expressed in an uncompromising love for "neighbors and strangers, friends and enemies."[12] A real Christian does all possible good for others: "Not only to their bodies, by 'feeding the hungry, clothing the naked, visiting those that are sick or in prison'; but much more does he labour to do good to their souls, as of the ability which God giveth; to awaken those that sleep in death; to bring those who are awakened to the atoning blood . . . and to provoke those who have peace with God to abound more in love and in good works" (Mt 25:35-36; also 2 Cor 9:8; Heb 10:24).

In Wesley's mind, Methodists simply shared the vocation of all real Christians by seeking to have their lives "inwardly and outwardly conformed to the will of God, as revealed in the written word."[13] Any true disciple, "thinks, speaks, and lives, according to the method laid down in the revelation of Jesus Christ . . . And having the mind that was in Christ, he so walks as Christ also walked." The pursuit of holiness is the imitation of Christ.

Pressing on to Perfection

Wesley reminded his readers that the subtitle to *The Character of a Methodist* was, "Not as though I had already attained."[14] This recalls the longings expressed by Paul in his letter to the Philippians, to know Christ more fully in the power of the resurrection and the fellowship of his sufferings (Phil 3:7-11). Paul said, "Not that I have already obtained all this or have already arrived at my goal . . . but I press on toward the goal to win the prize for which God has called me heavenward in Christ Jesus" (3:12-14). Real Christians are not distinguished by their attainments but by their aspirations.

Wesley did not claim to "describe what the Methodists are already, but what they desire to be, and what they will be then when they fully practice the doctrine they hear."[15] Whether some have attained perfection in love or not, real Christians are those who strive after it, and we need the help of others to keep "pressing on" in the life of discipleship. Paul insisted the Philippians should "join together in following my example, brothers and sisters, and just as you have us as a model, keep your eyes on those who live as we do" (Phil 3:17).

Wesley's teaching on Christian perfection attracted a lot of criticism, but perhaps the most crucial debate was whether we could be perfected in this life. Martin Luther argued that our discipleship would always be marred by sin until we escape our life in this fallen world. Wesley rejected this for three main reasons. First, it limits God's power to save us to the uttermost, and ultimately gives sin the final word in our lives. Second, Jesus came to reveal how human flesh could be perfected by grace, and we are called to have the fullness of his life through the power of his Spirit. Third, we are to hunger and thirst for the prize, because it is something that God longs to give.

When the early Methodist preachers failed to announce this great salvation in any place, the whole work of God suffered. Without vision, the people perish (Prov 29:18). The purpose of spiritual discipline is lost when we lose sight of the goal, and the life of discipleship is lost when discipline becomes an end in itself. In order to make whole-life and lifelong disciples, we must hold up a clear vision of spiritual maturity and provide the means for attaining it.[16]

THE NECESSITY OF SPIRITUAL DISCIPLINE

Wesley learned from the early church that "the soul and the body make a man" but "the Spirit and discipline make a Christian."[17] It was his own observation that "whatever doctrine is preached, where there is not discipline, it cannot have its full effect upon the hearers." The main problem with discipleship is not ignorance about what we should do. Lack of knowledge is easily solved by more preaching, teaching, and Bible studies. Even so, we can have all the best doctrine in our minds and still be devilish in our hearts (Jam 2:19). The real problem is that we just don't do what we know we should do. Jesus warned against being "a foolish man who built his house on sand," and James warned against finding our identity by looking in the "mirror" of Scripture, then walking away and forgetting who we are (Jam 1:22-24; also Mt 7:26; Gal 5:6). There is a gap between hearing and doing the word of God or between knowing and living the gospel, because we don't have a heart for true discipleship.

Wesley gave us two ways of diagnosing the problem.[18] First, we suffer from spiritual "dissipation," which he defines as "un-centering the soul from God" by the endless distractions of daily life. He said dissipation "is the parent of all sin." Second, we must contend with the "deceitfulness" of the human heart, which makes us wise in our own eyes. This tendency gives birth to sin and an endless capacity to justify our ungodliness. Through these weaknesses, the enemy of our souls labors with all his strength and subtlety to draw us away from the life of God and ensnare us in the ways of this world. The radical cure for dissipation and deception is submitting ourselves to the discipline of Christian fellowship and trusting ourselves to those "who have not yet bowed either their knee or their heart to the god of this world."[19]

The Problem of Solitary Christianity

Although George Whitefield first persuaded Wesley to preach in the fields, there arose a famous distinction between their respective methods of evangelism. Like many other revival evangelists of the time, it seems that Whitefield's preaching aimed at making converts but without an initial call to costly discipleship.[20] He was later to observe that "John, thou art in thy right place. My brother

Wesley acted wisely; the souls that were awakened under his ministry he joined in class, and thus preserved the fruits of his labour: this I neglected, and my people are a rope of sand."[21] For Wesley, the most important fruit of evangelistic preaching was not conversion as such, but awakening sinners to the need of salvation and salvation to the uttermost. Those who responded were initiated into a Methodist society; or, if needed, a new society was planted for the purpose. They were incorporated into class meetings as the primary means by which they pursued the whole way of salvation.

After traveling for several days in South Wales, at the heart of Calvinistic Methodism, Wesley wrote, "I was more convinced than ever, that the preaching like an Apostle without joining together those that are awakened and training them up in the ways of God is only begetting children for the murderer. How much preaching has there been for these twenty years all over Pembrokeshire! But no regular societies, no discipline, no order or connection; and the consequence is that nine in ten of the once-awakened are now faster asleep than ever."[22] Scripture warns that "your enemy the devil prowls around like a roaring lion looking for someone to devour"; and left to ourselves, we become easy prey (1 Pet 5:8). No matter where someone was on the way of salvation, it was a basic principle of early Methodism that he or she could not undertake the journey of discipleship alone.

Wesley was also disturbed by some forms of mysticism that taught that the spiritual journey was best undertaken alone by wrestling with sin in the depths of one's own heart. One thing that the gospel preachers and these mystics had in common was a belief that once the right foundations were laid, individuals could be left to build their own life of discipleship. Against this, Wesley claimed there is no such thing as solitary Christianity: "The gospel of Christ knows of no religion, but social; no holiness but social holiness."[23] In other words, the pursuit of holiness required the discipline of Christian fellowship found in societies, classes, and bands.

Drawing upon Hebrews 10, he urged the Methodists "not to forsake the assembling of yourselves together, as the manner of some is" but "to instruct, admonish, exhort, reprove, comfort, confirm, and every way build up one another" (see Heb 10:22-25).[24] Interestingly, this Scripture begins with an allusion to baptism, that "having our bodies washed with pure water" (10:22), we are to "hold unswervingly to the hope we profess" (10:23). Because of our tendency toward dissipation and deception, "swerving" from the way of Jesus is our problem. It is only by meeting together in fellowship that our course can be corrected, by "encouraging one another" and considering "how we may spur one another on toward love and good deeds" (10:24). Avoiding the discipline of Christian fellowship assures that our spiritual lives will crumble. Succumbing to privatized spirituality has always been a great spiritual force of wickedness in the church and never more so than today.

Real Christian Fellowship

By gathering people into societies, Wesley was accused by some of schism. In response, he argued that most Methodists had previously been unchurched parishioners with no true fellowship in the first place. "Who watched over them in love? Who marked their growth in grace? Who advised and exhorted them from time to time? Who prayed with them and for them, as they had need? This, and this alone, is Christian fellowship." Indeed, he argued that one would be hard pressed to find such fellowship anywhere else in England:

> "Are not the bulk of the parishioners a mere rope of sand? What Christian connection is there between them? What intercourse in spiritual things? What watching over each other's souls? What bearing of one another's burdens?

What a mere jest is it then, to talk so gravely of destroying what never was! The real truth is just the reverse of this: We introduce Christian fellowship where it was utterly destroyed. And the fruits of it have been peace, joy, love, and zeal for every good word and work."[25]

Here we have all the key qualities of disciplined Christian fellowship in the early Methodist movement. First, it promoted "Christian connection" or deep friendship in which people shared the journey of discipleship through all the challenges of daily life. Second, they had "intercourse in spiritual things," or spiritual conversation, in which they learned how to reflect on the presence and leading of God. Third, they "watched over each other's souls," holding one another accountable for their growth in grace and offering spiritual guidance. The need to watch and pray was a practice of vigilance in spiritual warfare, helping one another resist the temptation to give up the pursuit of holiness or give in to the powers of worldliness.

Wesley described the so-called fellowship in most churches as a mere "rope of sand." A rope of sand is nothing more than a collection of individual particles assembled to have the appearance of something it is not, and it easily falls apart. The analogy is clear. We don't get real Christian fellowship by gathering a bunch of self-centered individuals together at the same time and place for one hour on a Sunday morning. Such an assembly might have the appearance of being the church, but it is an illusion. That which binds us together as the people of God is deep spiritual friendship, conversation, and guidance. This was at the heart of every gathering in early Methodism, especially in the classes and bands. Wesley called these small groups "the sinews of our Society" that hold the body together, and without which "the most ardent attempts, by mere preaching, have proved of no lasting use."[26]

ORGANIZED TO BEAT THE DEVIL

It has been said that the early Methodist movement was organized to "beat the devil."[27] Wesley claimed the "prince of this world" fears real Christians and is even more afraid when "bodies of men are visibly united together with the avowed design to overthrow his kingdom."[28] This is what it means to fulfill our baptismal vows as disciples and as disciple-making communities.

Putting Ourselves to Death

A useful guide to baptism as a way of life and as a form of spiritual combat can be found in Wesley's *Collection of Forms of Prayer for Every Day in the Week.*[29] In the preface, he sets out five scriptural principles. They remind us of Jesus' command, "Whoever wants to be my disciple must deny themselves and take up their cross daily and follow me" (Lk 9:23). They also reflect Paul's teaching that taking up our cross means participating in the death and resurrection of Jesus on a daily basis.[30] Baptism by immersion is a symbol of this. Going down into the water, we are buried with Christ and put to death our sinful nature. Coming up from the water, we are raised to new life in Christ, so his nature can be formed in us. Wesley used the strange language of "mortification" to mean having our self-centered nature "gradually killed, by virtue of our union with him," so we can be renewed in the image of God.[31]

The first principle of discipleship is "renouncing ourselves." This means remembering we are not our own and being resolved to give up our self-centered ways. Second, this leads to "the devoting of ourselves to God," yielding all we have and are into his hands and living for his glory alone. Third, "self-denial" is a natural consequence as we struggle to resist the temptations of this world and submit to the purposes of God, no matter what the cost. Fourth, through this, the true disciple "continually advances in mortification" until we desire nothing but God. Fifth, we eventually come to say with Paul, "I am crucified unto the world; I am dead with Christ; I live not, but Christ liveth in me," as Savior and Lord (Gal 2:20, 6:14; Rom 6:11). This is the fulfilling of the law and the secret of Christian perfection. Wesley summarized, "He that being dead to the world is alive to God; the desire of whose soul is unto his name; who has given Him his whole heart; who delights in Him, and in nothing else but what tends to Him; who, for his sake, burns with love to all mankind." These are what Scupoli called the "weapons without which it is impossible to gain the victory in this spiritual combat."[32]

Wesley reminds us that "the end of Christ's coming" was to destroy the work of the devil.[33] Jesus accomplished this in life by plundering the kingdom of Satan, and in death by disarming the principalities and powers through the cross (Mt 12:22-29; Col 2:15). Scripture teaches us that Jesus shared our humanity "so that by his death he might break the power of him who holds the power of death—that is, the devil" (Heb 2:14). By remembering our baptism, we take up our cross daily and also share in his victory over the powers of sin and death. "Submit yourselves, then, to God. Resist the devil, and he will flee from you" (Jam 4:7).

Wesley's pattern of morning and evening prayer, together with questions for self-examination, guides the reader through one of the above themes each day. This begins on Sunday with reflecting on God's love for us that we might love him back with all our heart, mind, soul, and strength: "May this holy flame ever warm my breast, that I may serve thee with all my might; and let it consume in my heart all selfish desires."[34] Monday continues with prayers for laying down our lives in love of neighbor: "Let thy love to me, O blessed Saviour, be the pattern of my love"[35] to others. Putting our pride and selfish desires to death are the themes for Tuesday and Wednesday, so we might have purity of heart and live faithfully to the purposes of God in our lives: "Let it be the one desire of my heart, to be as my Master; to do, not my own will, but the will of Him that sent me."[36] Thursday picks up the theme of resignation found in the practice of covenant renewal: "O Lord Jesu, I give thee my body, my soul, my substance, my fame, my friends, my liberty, my life: Dispose of me, and all that is mine, as it seemeth best unto thee. I am not mine, but thine; Claim me as thy right, keep me as thy charge, love me as thy child! Fight for me when I am assaulted, heal me when I am wounded, and revive me when I am destroyed."[37]

Friday is a day of fasting and prayer through which we confront the evil powers of this world: "Savior of the world . . . destroy the power of the devil in me." We ask Jesus to "cast out of my heart all corrupt affections" that dissipate and deceive my soul. "Open my eyes, and fix them singly on the prize of my high calling, and cleanse my heart from every desire but that of advancing thy glory."[38] Finally, the theme for Saturday is thanksgiving for the goodness of God and making our whole lives an act of spiritual worship: "O pour thy grace into my heart, that I may worthily magnify thy great and glorious name . . . Guide me by thy Holy Spirit in all those places whither thy providence shall lead me this day" that I might not be "lukewarm in thy service . . . O that I had the heart of the seraphim, that I might burn with love like theirs."[39]

Fasting and prayer on Friday, in anticipation of Lord's Supper on Sunday, was also a way of journeying with Jesus through the three days of Easter. We might interpret Wesley's practice of "constant communion" as a primary liturgical means of remembering our baptism.[40]

Putting Each Other to Death

Yet the truth is, we cannot put our old selves to death by ourselves. The text of Wesley's prayer for Friday evening makes this plain: "Sanctify, O merciful Lord, the friendship which thou hast granted me with these thy servants . . . Let our prayers be heard for each other, while our hearts are united in thy fear and love, and graciously unite them therein more and more. Strengthen the hearts of us thy servants against all our corruptions and temptations; enable us to consecrate ourselves faithfully and entirely to thy service." It is through fellowship that we stay connected with Jesus, and from this "spiritual, vital union with him, proceeds the influence of his grace on those that are baptized."[41] In other words, Christian fellowship is a means of grace.

Wesley tells us there are always two kinds of power at work in the world.[42] There is a "mystery of godliness" in which the "sanctifying Spirit" draws all humanity to Jesus from a life of darkness into the light of his kingdom. Alongside this, however, is the "mystery of iniquity" that undermines the sanctifying mission of God by infusing a love of the world. This "energy of Satan" captivates people's hearts and lives to habits of sinfulness.

The church has been called to reveal the mystery of godliness in the world through lives that overcome the powers of sin and death (Eph 3:10). But the mystery of iniquity works subversively among us to dissipate our spiritual lives and deceive us into settling for worldliness. Meeting in Christian fellowship is a way of living on the front line between the sanctifying power of the Spirit and the worldly power of Satan in our own hearts and in the life of the church. Wesley observed that the great objection of the world to Christianity is the lives of Christians and how great is the "watchfulness they need who desire to be real Christians; considering what a state the world is in."[43]

Watchfulness is not merely a solitary discipline of self-examination, but the essence of real fellowship. The great purpose of Methodist society was uniting people to "watch over one another in love." Historically speaking, this responsibility has belonged to those in pastoral leadership of the church.[44] Wesley simply defined a pastor as a "spiritual guide" who helps us in the pursuit of holiness and whose own life is worthy of imitation. He said we should submit to those who live in conformity to the word of God and use it for "teaching, rebuking, correcting and training in righteousness" (2 Tim 3:16). But who are our pastors, the guides of our souls? The answer for Wesley was not merely those formally appointed over us in the church but also the spiritual friends we make in small-group fellowship.

It may be the responsibility of church leaders to perform baptisms, but it is the responsibility of the whole church to make disciples by guiding one another in the life of discipleship. Just as a new believer submits to baptism at the hands of a pastor, so we must submit to the sanctifying work of God by placing our lives in the hands of our friends. From a Wesleyan perspective, we remember our baptism by regular immersion in a fellowship of spiritual guides who help us die to ourselves and become alive to God. Through mutual submission, accountability, and spiritual guidance, we help one another take up our cross and overcome the enemy of our souls.

Putting Our Congregations to Death

One sure sign that the mystery of iniquity is at work in the church is a lack of self-denial and a resistance to spiritual discipline. Where this occurs, church members tend to hide behind a veil of private spirituality and only tolerate leaders who serve as therapists or chaplains to their self-centered lives. Wesley implored the church to resist this weakening of spiritual leadership saying, "It is not enough for a Minister of the gospel not to oppose the doctrine of self-denial."[45] Rather, "he must inculcate the necessity of it in the clearest and strongest manner; he must press it with his might, on all persons, at all times, and in all places." Only then, "shall he save his own soul and those that hear him."

Spiritual leadership means assisting congregations to remember their baptism by holding them under the water and inviting God to finish the work of putting their sinful habits to death. Wesley viewed the broad resistance among Protestants to "obey and submit" to spiritual guides as a serious failure of discipleship. Effective leadership in the Wesleyan tradition will equip the whole church for the ministry of watching over one another's souls through the discipline of Christian fellowship. In this way, it may be organized to beat the devil.

REMEMBERING OUR BAPTISM

I am aware that almost everything I have said in this chapter may seem scandalous. All this ancient talk about spiritual warfare is a bit far fetched for our enlightened ears. The very idea of voluntary submission to spiritual guides has become offensive to those raised in a culture of autonomous individualism and privatized spirituality. The whole scheme of denying ourselves just sounds like some kind of spiritual abuse to those trained in the prevailing dogmas of self-esteem. Of course, if there is no spiritual battle, then there is no need for disciplined fellowship. But if we are in a spiritual battle, our cultured disbelief is itself a work of the enemy.[46] Either way, remembering our baptism should cause us to reflect on our vows to fight the good fight.

- **Initiation into the life of discipleship**. Reflecting on our baptismal vows should awaken us to the true nature of discipleship as spiritual warfare. We may be assailed from within and without, but the good news is, God wins. Jesus overcame the powers of evil in his earthly ministry and finally conquered them through his death and resurrection. If we share in his battle, we also share in his victory. Are

we prepared to take our vows seriously by coming to terms
with the worldliness in our own hearts and in the life of the
church? If so, we may have to face our captivity to sin along
with our lack of training for the fight.

- **Dedication to the pursuit of holiness.** To confess Jesus as
  our Savior means inviting his Spirit to save us to the uttermost, from both the guilt and the power of sin. And to take
  Jesus as Lord means becoming a co-worker with his Spirit so
  that we may be changed into his likeness from the inside out.
  Are we prepared to take our vows seriously by committing to
  the pursuit of holiness? For this is the key to discipleship and
  mission, as well as the connection between them. Only by
  seeking the perfection of love are we trained to give up our
  whole heart to God and lay down our whole life for others.

- **Participation in the mission of God.** Pledging allegiance
  to Jesus in baptism also means sharing in his battle to overcome evil in the world. For some of us, that might mean
  wrestling with strongholds of local and national politics. But
  for all of us, it means attending to the brokenness and need
  of our neighbors down the street, in the workplace, and the
  church. Are we prepared to take our vows seriously by living as agents of the kingdom? We deal the greatest blow to
  the powers of evil when we share the gospel, make new disciples, and baptize them into the life of true discipleship.

- **Collaboration in disciple-making fellowship.** As we
  take up our cross through the discipline of Christian fellowship, the Spirit will set us free from the powers of sin and
  death. It is only with the help of spiritual friends that we can
  answer the above questions positively and with any degree
  of confidence. So, the key question is: "Are we prepared to
  take our vows seriously by training for this battle and engaging the fight as a fellowship of 'spiritual warriors'?" Because
  we know that our conflict is not against flesh and blood,

we do not take up the weapons of violence but the ways of peaceful engagement. Remember that we are fighting for the reign of God's love to prevail in our own lives and to spread throughout the world.

In the next chapter we will look more closely at what it means to be baptized into the church as a community of disciples who bear witness to the kingdom of God against the powers of this world. We will see how our life together in the church is a revelation of the gospel and a place of spiritual formation for mission. And we will see why being such a community is essential for any practice of baptism, but especially for those who baptize infants.

Questions for Further Reflection

1. After reading this chapter, how have your views changed about the nature of Christian fellowship and why it is necessary for discipleship?

2. What is your vision for the kind of life you are called to pursue as a disciple? How do you respond to the idea of discipleship as the pursuit of perfection?

3. Why might it be helpful to think about discipleship as a spiritual battle? Do you ever feel like you are battling with "principalities and powers"?

4. In what ways are you tempted to settle for solitary Christianity? Why must we depend on fellowship with others if we are to live as real Christians?

5. Which parts of the fourfold pattern for remembering our baptism at the conclusion of this chapter do you find the most challenging? How is the Spirit guiding you?

CHAPTER 8

The Witness of a Holy People

With God's help we will proclaim the good news and live according to the example of Christ. We will surround these persons with a community of love and forgiveness, that they may grow in their trust of God, and be found faithful in their service to others. We will pray for them, that they may be true disciples who walk in the way that leads to life.[1]

Remembering our baptism means belonging to a community of disciples whose life together bears witness to the counter-cultural reality of the kingdom. Are you part of a community whose love for one another is a light in the world?

Baptism is an initiation into the life of discipleship through initiation into the community of the church.[2] But what sort of community are we entering? One way to answer this question is by reflecting on the promises made by the local church to those who are being baptized. First, the church promises to proclaim the gospel and live as good examples for people to follow. Second, the congregation promises to be a community of love and forgiveness, among whom people might grow in grace and faith. Third, the congregation promises to pray they might live as whole-life and lifelong disciples. In short, the church vows to be a community that will help people grow to maturity in the life of discipleship and mission.

In this chapter, we will reflect more deeply on these vows by developing Wesley's thoughts on social holiness as a description of our life together as the church. The social nature of holiness means our discipleship must be worked out in the company and conversation of others. From this perspective, Wesley's vision of holiness encompasses two ways of being the church in the world. At certain times, the church is gathered out of the world as the family of God for worship and witness to his love in our life together. Most of the time, however, the church is scattered into the world, where we each must live as witnesses to the love of God in the relationships and encounters of everyday life. Baptism initiates us into a rhythm of community marked by this gathering and scattering.

Some Wesleyan scholars have observed the parallels between early Methodism and the Anabaptist tradition of radical Christianity with its strong emphasis on disciple-making community.[3] We will explore some points of comparison between them and reflect on what it means to remember our baptism as a holy people committed to the task of making disciples.

RADICAL CHRISTIANITY

The Anabaptist movement emerged during the Protestant Reformation of the early sixteenth century.[4] Although the reformers had won major battles in relation to church doctrine, government, and worship, they had done little to reform the discipleship of ordinary people. It was this deficiency that the Anabaptists labored to correct, and they were called radicals for a number of reasons. First, they patterned their life on the radical teaching of Jesus in his Sermon on the Mount and took the Pentecost community described in Acts as a model for the church. Second, they were radical in their unwillingness to settle for nominal Christianity, looking to the power of the Spirit for strength to follow Jesus and bear witness to his kingdom in the whole of life. Third, this uncompromising discipleship was expressed by planting communities that stood against the powers of worldliness, both in the state and its established churches.

It is not surprising that the radicals were persecuted. They were a threat to the stability of the newly reformed state churches, and they were intent on spreading their dissenting ideas wherever they went. Among other things, they rejected the practice of infant baptism because it had been co-opted by the state as a mark of good citizenship, while perpetuating the problem of nominal Christianity. They were called "Anabaptists" because they initiated people into the movement through believer's baptism as a sign of personal conversion to the way of Jesus. Although many converts had already been baptized as infants, they considered this immersion to be a first true baptism as fully committed disciples. The state considered it to be rebaptism and an act of civil disobedience.[5] It was likely to get them hunted down, imprisoned, tortured, and killed.

In his book, *The Radical Wesley*, Howard Snyder claims that Wesley's leadership may be likened to the Anabaptists in that he "worked ceaselessly for a more vital, more aggressive, more loving, and more authentically visible manifestation of the church as the community of God's people, the eschatological community which was to be the agent now of the coming Kingdom of God."[6] We will delve a bit deeper into these themes before seeing how they relate to the early Methodist movement, including the question of infant baptism.

Living in the Shadow of Christendom

We have seen how the Methodist movement had much in common with the early Christians and their approach to making disciples in a hostile culture. The big difference is that Methodism emerged within the social arrangements of Christendom and had to contend with the nominal Christianity of a worldly church. In this respect, the Anabaptists and Methodists shared a similar missional context, and their response to it makes them cousins under the skin.

Being baptized as a Christian in the early church meant initiation into a community of radical discipleship that set them at odds with the principalities and powers of the world. After the so-called conversion of Emperor Constantine, all this changed. Christianity could spread more freely and became the official religion of the Roman Empire (in 380 CE) under the rule of Emperor Theodosius I.[7] Christendom was born, and from that time, the radical difference between church and world was gradually erased. The world became nominally Christian, and the church became evermore worldly. Anabaptist theologians refer to this as the "Constantinian synthesis."

Throughout the medieval period, the pursuit of holiness was exemplified by religious orders of monks and mystics, cloistered away from the routines of daily life in the world. The Reformation may have put biblical truth in the hands of ordinary people, but it did not challenge the Constantinian synthesis itself. Discipleship was still confused with good citizenship, and the church remained a department of state. This arrangement was eventually challenged by the rise of dissenting movements such as the Puritan and Pietist forebears of early Methodism.

With the advance of enlightenment individualism, the modern world became even less outwardly Christian, while the faith became increasingly privatized. A natural consequence of this has been the evolution of postmodern pluralism. The world is now a melting pot of competing claims to truth. Good citizenship demands that personal faith must be concealed as a matter of private opinion in order to keep the peace. We have been turned into spiritual consumers and, wittingly or unwittingly, the church has been tempted to accept its new role as purveyor of religious services in exchange for member loyalty. But despite the best efforts of church growth experts to help us be more effective in "marketing" the gospel, the membership statistics of our denominations are still in free fall.[8]

It is widely agreed that we now live in a post-Christendom society, yet the Christendom mindset still lingers.[9] This is especially true where the church sees its main task as Christianizing the world by accommodating to its fashions in order to be more relevant and attractive. This may seem like a desirable and missional strategy, reflecting the principles of incarnation and contextualization, but we really cannot address the task of mission without confronting the problem of worldliness in the church. As our culture divests itself of Christian values with ever-increasing rapidity, the danger of accommodation lies in abandoning the call to scriptural holiness. The more we fail to pursue a visibly different way of life, the more irrelevant we actually become in a world that has decided to do without even nominal Christianity.

The Anabaptist tradition has always understood that holiness is a missional issue. It means living as a countercultural witness to the presence of the kingdom in a world of unbelief. It means being the kind of community whose way of life makes sense of the invitation to become a disciple.[10] True faith in Jesus will always be more of a problem than a help to people intent on pursuing secularized lifestyles, especially those in the church. But for those unbelievers who are tired of being abused by the powers of worldliness, a visible alternative might actually present hope for real change. Such people are not looking for private spirituality or nominal religion.[11] They are looking for an authentic way of life that displays a real faith in Jesus. The early church knew this, as did the Anabaptists, the Methodists, and all those who have pursued radical Christianity through the ages.

The Church as a Community of Disciples

The church gathers to be nurtured, equipped, and strengthened for living as a faithful witness to the kingdom of God. Peter reminds us, "You are a chosen people, a royal priesthood, a holy nation, God's special possession, that you may declare the praises of him who called you out of darkness into his wonderful light" (1 Pet 2:9). The tradition of radical Christianity has often drawn out these themes to explain what it means to be a community of disciples on mission with God.[12]

We are a "chosen people." The church has inherited the vocation of Israel to live in covenant relationship with God as his people in the world. Jesus reminded his disciples, "You did not choose me, but I chose you and appointed you so that you might go and bear fruit" (Jn 15:16). Like Israel, they were not chosen because they deserved it, nor were they chosen for the sake of privilege. Rather, they were chosen to live a way of life that declares the praises of God in a world of unbelief.

We are a "royal priesthood." The church lives in this covenant with God as a forgiven people who are called to the ministry of reconciliation. Jesus commissioned his disciples to share in this ministry: "As the Father has sent me, I am sending you . . . If you forgive anyone's sins, their sins are forgiven" (Jn 20:23). Here is the priesthood of all believers. It is not simply that we serve as "priests" to one another, but that the church participates in the mission of Jesus to bring all people into a saving relationship with God.

We are a "holy nation." The church is commanded to be holy, set apart from worldliness as a witness to the kingdom of God. Jesus told his disciples, "Be perfect, therefore, as your heavenly Father is perfect" (Mt 5:48). The church is holy, because Jesus stands in our midst and his Spirit renews the image of God among us. The word "nation" really just means a "people group" that has its own language and culture. So, the life of the church can be thought of as an alternative culture, set apart from the life of the nations of this world and their false gods.

We are a "special possession." This recalls the covenant imagery of marriage and the zealous love of God for his people. Jesus said, "You do not belong to the world, but I have chosen you out of the world" to bear much fruit (Jn 15:19). The clearest sign that we have been seduced by the powers of worldliness is when the church is torn apart by selfish ambition, bitterness, jealousy, factions, evil speaking, and unforgiveness. Only when we are repossessed by the power of the Spirit will we be healed and produce the fruit of "love, joy, peace, forbearance, kindness, goodness, faithfulness, gentleness and self-control" (Gal 5:19-26; also Eph 4:17-32).

Finally, we are "light" in the darkness. The church takes up the original calling of Israel to be a light among the nations (Is 51:4, 60:1-3). Jesus said to his disciples, "You are the light of the world. A city built on a hill cannot be hidden . . . In the same way, let your light shine before others, that they may see your good deeds and glorify your Father in heaven" (Mt 5:14, 16). A city (Greek, *polis*, from which we get the English word, "politics") is a whole community of people, governed by a common way of life. When the church is governed by the teaching and "politics of Jesus," the reality of the kingdom will shine brightly, and people will be drawn to its beauty.[13] The community of discipleship is itself God's mission project in the world. From the first church born at Pentecost until today, it is our way of life, both gathered and scattered, that makes the gospel attractive to unbelievers.

The Church as a Disciple-Making Community

There is an African proverb that says, "It takes a village to raise a child." Children cannot raise themselves, and their parents cannot raise them alone. The word "village" is derived from the Latin, *villaticum*, which can be translated, a "community of houses," perhaps in the form of a "farmstead." A village is a rural community that works on the land to cultivate the soil and make it fruitful for the good of everyone. Children have to be apprenticed in the ways of the village, by precept and example, if they are going to share its values and become fruitful members of the community.

Radical Christianity throughout the ages has understood that "it takes a church to raise a Christian."[14] The analogy is plain. The church needs a culture of discipleship if it is going to make true followers of Jesus (Mt 7:15-29). Discipleship is a way of life that can only be nurtured by a community that is intentional about obedience to the teaching of Jesus and cultivating the fruit of his Spirit in their life together. In short, we can make disciples only by apprenticing one another in the disciplines of Christian fellowship.

The Anabaptist tradition has typically looked to the Sermon on the Mount as a curriculum for discipleship and a manifesto for kingdom community. Starting with the Beatitudes (Mt 5:1-12), Jesus taught his disciples what a community of the kingdom should look like: A community of the "poor in spirit" that has given up selfish ambition and finds its hope in God alone. A community of "mourners" that has given up trying to predict and control its own future and trusts itself into the hands of God. A community of "meekness" that has given up the desire to choose its own way and submits to the reign of God in all things. A community that "hungers and thirsts for righteousness" that has given up seeking satisfaction in this world and longs to see the kingdom of God come in its midst. A community of "mercy" that has given up being driven by greed and chooses to love as it has been loved by God. A community of "pure hearts" that has given up chasing after the latest fashions and has set its desires on seeing and following the work of God. A community of "peacemakers" that has given up trying to capitalize on the brokenness of others and seeks to establish healing relationships with God at the center. A community of "persecuted" followers that has given up expecting to make peace with the powers of this world and trusts that the battle belongs to the Lord.

Jesus then took the law of Moses and showed his community of disciples its truly radical meaning as a call to holiness that would make them a light in the world (Mt 5:21-48). You have heard it said, "You shall not murder," but in a world of aggression and violence, you must not even be angry because God is perfect peace. You have heard it said, "You shall not commit adultery," but in a world filled with infidelity and immorality, you must not even succumb to lust because God is perfect faithfulness. You have heard it said, "Do not swear falsely," but in a world of suspicion and distrust, you must not even make oaths with one another because God is perfect truthfulness. You have heard it said, "An eye for an eye and a tooth for a tooth," but in a world of revenge and retaliation, you must turn the other cheek because God is perfect forgiveness. Finally, you have heard it said, "Hate your enemy," but in a world of intolerance and persecution, you must love even your enemies because God is perfect love.

Jesus was not just trying to establish a social experiment with values different from those of the world. He was describing a way of life that would reveal the very presence and nature of God in their life together (Mt 6:19-34). It is a way of life that flows from the reign of God in our hearts and establishes the kingdom of God through our lives and relationships. Jesus was teaching his disciples how to live as citizens of the kingdom, even though it would set them at odds with the world and be very costly to pursue. Like them, we must choose between the love of God and the love of "money," or living in the light and remaining in the darkness. Choosing to walk in the light will mean learning to live without fear by trusting that God will provide and protect, no matter what hardship or persecution we face. We must persevere in prayer, asking especially for the gift of the Spirit to empower us for his kingdom purposes. "Our Father in heaven, hallowed be your name, your kingdom come, your will be done, on earth as it is in heaven." Let it begin with us (Mt 6:1-16; also 7:7-12; Lk 11:11-13).

Belonging to a Radical Christian Community

Jesus said, "where two or three gather in my name, there am I with them" (Mt 18:20). He made this promise while laying out a simple process for exercising discipline in the community. If someone sins against you, seek to resolve it personally. If that fails, take one or two others along. If the person still does not listen, take it to the whole church. When all else fails, this person must be treated as "a pagan or a tax collector." Unrepentant sinners have effectively set themselves out of covenant relationship with God and his people.

The Anabaptists emphasize this community discipline as the practice of "binding and loosing."[15] The community binds one another to the teaching of Jesus and holds one another accountable for living in accordance with it. They also have the authority to loose people from the obligations of discipleship and their covenant responsibilities. It should be noted that this process is intended to be restorative, not punitive, with the goal of forgiveness and reconciliation (Jn 20:22-23; also Jn 16:13; Mt 6:14-15; Eph 4:32; Col 3:13). Treating unrepentant sinners as pagans is not to abandon them, but to view them as lost sheep that we must bring back into the fold (Mt 18:10-14). The purpose of binding and loosing is ultimately a disciple-making practice of missional community.

Discipleship implies a personal decision to become a follower of Jesus and to be apprenticed by his community. Jesus has promised to be present through the power of his Spirit who will remind us of his teaching and guide us into all truth. From this perspective, baptism should be seen as an act of binding ourselves to Jesus through submission to the disciplines of Christian fellowship. Obviously, infants cannot make this decision. But it is the obligation of all who are baptized, at whatever age, to embrace such discipline, and the baptizing community vows to provide it. John Howard Yoder notes that there can be "no renewal of the church without it" and that "movements of renewal, from Pietism to John Wesley to the present, have restored in one way or another this model of loving dialogue." He goes on to note that "the 'classes' and 'bands' of Wesley's age performed this function," combining "the substance of moral discernment, and the authority of divine empowerment."[16] Let us now explore this observation a bit further.

SOCIAL HOLINESS

Because of the lingering Christendom mindset, Wesley's concept of social holiness has generally been misunderstood or half-interpreted. On the one hand, it has been taken to mean the task of making wider society more holy or Christianizing the world. This is not what Wesley intended. On the other hand, "society" has been interpreted to mean the disciplines of Christian fellowship that empower individuals to pursue holiness of heart and life. This is certainly part of Wesley's argument against the inwardness of mysticism and the problem of "solitary Christianity." But there is still a danger that small groups will turn inward and be reduced to study groups or therapeutic huddles.

Nearly a third of Wesley's standard *Sermons on Several Occasions* is dedicated to his commentary on the Sermon on the Mount.[17] His explanation of social holiness comes in his exposition of Matthew 5:13-16, on being salt and light in world.[18] In other words, it is a way of speaking about how we participate in the mission of God as a tangible witness to the kingdom.[19] There was the witness of Methodist society as a gathered community of disciples, rooted in the form of life they shared together. And there was the witness of real Christians formed by this disciple-making community and scattered into the social realities of daily life. First, let us outline the problem that Wesley was trying to address.

The State of the Church

Paul urged the church "to live a life worthy of the calling you have received" (Eph 4:1-6). For Wesley, the church was meant to be a community of disciples who "walk worthy" of Jesus and is being transformed into his likeness from the inside out. From this perspective, he notes that gatherings as small as house fellowships or even a Christian family can be thought of as "church." Either way, the church is called holy, "because every member thereof is holy, though in different degrees, as He that called them is holy." This means being a community of disciples "endued with living faith," made visible in their life together.[20]

Wesley reminded the Methodists,

> "'Ye are the light of the world!' Ye are 'a city set upon a hill,' and 'cannot be hid.' O 'let your light shine before men!' Show them your faith by your works. Let them see, by the whole tenor of your conversation, that your hope is all laid up above! Let all your words and actions evidence the spirit whereby you are animated! Above all things, let your love abound. Let it extend to every child of man: Let it overflow to every child of God. By this let all men know whose disciples ye are, because you 'love one another.'"[21]

This is social holiness. But Wesley argued this vision of genuine Christianity was fatally wounded "in the fourth century by Constantine the Great, when he called himself a Christian, and poured in a flood of riches, honours, and power upon the Christians."[22] He clearly sides with the Anabaptists by arguing that Constantine's formulation of Christendom was the fall of the church, not the coming of Zion. From that time, "the Church and State, the kingdoms of Christ and of the world, were so strangely and unnaturally blended together" that so-called Christians could not be distinguished from their un-baptized neighbors.[23] Even the

Reformation was a failure because it addressed only the outward circumstances of religion, not the pursuit of holiness and witness.

Being Salt and Light

There can be no such thing as solitary Christianity, because the life of discipleship is inherently relational. The Great Commandment reminds us that we grow in the love of God only as that love is worked out with our neighbor. Similarly, having the peace of God in our souls means becoming a peacemaker and living at peace with others. Indeed, we cannot claim to have any fruit of the Spirit in our lives unless we are also humble, patient, kind, good, and faithful in all our relationships. The fruit is intentionally cultivated in Christian fellowship but grows to maturity only in relationship with people in the world, among friends, strangers, and even enemies. Wesley said, "This is the great reason why the providence of God has so mingled you together with other men, that whatever grace you have received of God may through you be communicated to others."[24] This is what it means to be the salt of the earth and a light in the world.

Social holiness is a relational witness to the grace of God in our lives and the beauty of holiness in a world of sin and death. There can be no such thing as solitary Christianity, and there can be no such thing as private spirituality. Wesley himself faced objections raised by the late Christendom mindset. Some asked, "May we not convey this into others in a secret and almost imperceptible manner?" So, "although we do not go out of the world, yet we may lay hid in it. We may thus keep our religion to ourselves; and not offend those whom we cannot help." Wesley called this the "reasoning of flesh and blood . . . so long as true religion abides in our hearts, it is impossible to conceal it," except by ceasing to be salty, or putting our light out. He concluded, "A secret, unobserved religion, cannot be the religion of Jesus Christ."[25] We need to hear this all the more in a post-Christendom context that is increasingly hostile to the faith and intent on silencing our witness.

Friendship with the World

Another clue to the meaning of social holiness is being *in* the world but not *of* the world (Jn 17:15-16). James warned "that friendship with the world means enmity against God" (Jam 4:4). Wesley observed that our spiritual life tended to dissipate through "friendship with the world" and urged us to avoid unnecessary attachment to unbelievers.[26] The intimacy required of true friendship should be reserved for those who help us "on our way to heaven." Wesley's caution does not focus on the good or evil intentions of unbelievers as such, but draws attention to the powers of worldliness at work among them. He likens this power to a contagious disease that creeps upon us by stealth and gradually dampens our zeal for God by increasing our desire for the things of this world. The enemy of our souls works in a "secret and unobserved manner" by dulling our spiritual senses, creating an indifference toward godliness, and finally captivating us to worldly pursuits even "before we are sensible of his attack" or "conscious of our loss."[27]

Wesley's caution does not entail withdrawing from the world or being indifferent toward the people of the world. The providence of God has placed us in the world with myriad personal relationships for the purpose of loving our neighbor. We must bear them goodwill, desire their happiness, encourage "all the good that is in them," and honor them as creatures made capable of fellowship with God.[28] For Wesley, then, our posture toward the world is not one of friendship as such, but of witness and mission. Ultimately, his warning is against friendship with the principalities and powers, not against loving relationships with broken humanity.

Wesley argued that we do not take leave of the world by retreating to the desert, or turning in upon ourselves, or hiding out in public. Rather, we are set apart by the pursuit of holiness and by visibly living the gospel in a world of unbelief. So, we might commend the idea of building relationships with unbelievers from a confidence that the beauty of holiness is more compelling than the lure of worldliness. To put it another way, Christian witness might be a more powerful contagion than earthly temptations. But we should remember that even relational evangelism is a power encounter that comes with a health warning: "If you do not raise their hearts to heaven, they will draw yours down to earth."[29] The question is, "How do we become a holy people who live as salt and light in the world?"

KINGDOM COMMUNITY

Social holiness was expressed through an expanding network of relationships from private households to Methodist society as the "household of faith" and then out into the world. We will briefly examine how the Christian family and the Methodist society both functioned as radical communities of discipleship and disciple making.

The Christian Household

Wesley's teaching on family religion started with the declaration of Joshua, "As for me and my household, we will serve the Lord" (Josh 24:15). This brings us back to the theme of covenant renewal and the need to choose between serving the Lord or giving up our lives to other gods. For Wesley, to serve meant the pursuit of holy love for God and neighbor. The household was an extended family that included any servants or visitors, and householders must watch over them as those "entrusted to your care, that you may train them up in all holiness."[30] In other words, the home is a context for making disciples on the front line of daily life where the competition for our souls is experienced most forcefully. Parents must not surrender their children to the powers of worldliness by preferring that they "grow more rich than more holy." By fostering a culture of service in the household, he warned, "You will have all the powers of darkness against you . . . and, above all, the deceitfulness of your own heart." So, "Go on in the name of the Lord, and in the power of his might!"[31]

Wesley required the obedience of children to their parents, not as an end in itself, but as a training in discipleship. He said, "It is by habituating them to your will" that you overcome their self-willed nature and "prepare them for submitting to the will of their Father which is in heaven." The parent who subdues self-will in their children "works together with God in the saving of a soul"; but "the parent who indulges it does the Devil's work." This method is only effective if parents teach by example, demonstrating the kind of obedience to God that they expect from their own children.[32] What is more, the only way parents will have lives worthy of imitation is if they are properly nurtured in the household of faith.

The Household of Faith

The *General Rules* gave shape to social holiness in the Methodist movement, and they were used by the classes and bands as a curriculum of accountability for individual discipleship. The discipline of Christian fellowship was a catalyst for the establishment of Methodist societies whose life together was a tangible witness to the kingdom of God. Each society became an alternative social reality, a countercultural witness against the powers of worldliness. They were successful in raising up ordinary people as political activists who confronted the social, economic, and political injustices of their time. Following the example of Wesley, they spoke out against moral dissipation, the plight of the poor, and the institutions of slavery. Even more important, the life of a Methodist society itself was a form of social action that gave credibility to their wider efforts, and they were persecuted for it. They were not persecuted because of a few notable radicals but because God was raising up a whole movement of radical Christianity that threatened the dominant social arrangements of the nation.

The first *General Rule* of doing no harm formed a society of resistance to the powers of sin and evil. They challenged a culture of moral dissipation by helping one another keep the Sabbath and abstain from drunkenness and violence. They challenged a culture of economic greed by helping one another to live frugally, avoid debt, reject usury, and resist the temptations to accumulate wealth and possessions. They challenged a culture of deceitful politics by helping one another speak truthfully in business and by refusing to overcome the weak through litigation.

The second *General Rule* of doing all possible good formed a society of co-workers in the kingdom. They helped one another lay down their lives in works of mercy to meet the needs of others, no matter what the cost. They helped one another redeem the usefulness of money by earning all they could and giving all they could to the household of faith. They helped one another in business and made a priority of employing the poor in their midst.

This was social holiness. Every member of the society was committed to the same *Rules*, "all which we are taught of God to observe, even in his written word," and which "his Spirit writes on every truly awakened heart."[33] Any member of society that broke them would be subject to the discipline of binding and loosing set out by Jesus. Wesley explained, "We will admonish him of the error of his ways; we will bear with him for a season," but "if he repent not, he hath no more place among us."

REMEMBERING OUR BAPTISM

From the perspective of radical Christianity, baptism represents a voluntary commitment to the life of social holiness when gathered in the community of disciples and scattered in the everyday world. The Anabaptists rejected infant baptism because young children could not make that decision for themselves. The discipline of Christian fellowship in early Methodism, however, provided a way for those baptized as infants to make such a personal commitment. But as Methodism made the transition to a separate denomination, it ceased to be a voluntary movement of radical Christianity and adopted the inclusivist stance of the Christendom mindset. Today, infants are baptized by churches that have generally lost the radical vision for social holiness and are no longer communities of authentic discipleship. This begs the question whether infant baptism is compatible with the pursuit of radical Christianity and recovering the spirit of a holiness movement.[34] Here are four ways we might continue to affirm the practice, all of which require churches to become radical communities of discipleship and disciple making. These principles get to the heart of what it means to disciple our children, whether we practice infant or believer's baptism.

- **Initiation into the life of discipleship**. It makes no sense baptizing either infants or new believers unless the church is committed to social holiness as the household of faith and helping parents turn their homes into places of spiritual formation. Assuming this is the case, I suggest we should baptize infants only because we know there is a competition for their souls. The world makes its claim upon our children from the moment they are born, and in baptism we make a counter-claim that they belong to the kingdom of God. Baptism is a sign of faith that God will have the last word in their lives, no matter what challenges we all may face in the future. The question is, "Are we content to let the world raise our children in its ways, or will we be the kind of community that will raise them in the ways of Jesus?"

- **Dedication to the pursuit of holiness.** By nature, we are born with a tendency toward self-centeredness and a vulnerability to the temptations of worldliness. Since baptism is a sign of dying and rising with Christ, we might view the baptism of infants as an invitation for the Spirit to put their selfish nature to death so they might grow up as children of God. Susanna Wesley's infamous approach to "breaking the will" of a child must be understood from this perspective. It does not mean crushing their self-esteem, but it does mean fulfilling the vows made at baptism to free them from bondage to sin so they can freely choose to serve God for themselves. The question is, "Are we ready to count the cost of helping our children become true disciples by denying themselves and taking up their cross daily?"

- **Participation in the mission of God.** When the Anabaptists refused to baptize their children, it was seen as a mark of civil disobedience. Ironically, under the conditions of post-Christendom, leaving children unbaptized can be seen as a mark of good citizenship in a secularized culture. Indeed, we might view infant baptism today as a practice of radical Christianity that sets us at odds with the world. In that case, baptism is the sign of a community intent on "radicalizing" its children by helping them grow as disciples who are prepared to live and die for Jesus. The question is, "Are we committed to living counterculturally in the church, so our children might be strengthened to resist the powers of this world and grow up as citizens of heaven?"

- **Collaboration in disciple-making fellowship.** Parents might baptize their children because they know the world will not raise them as Christians and because they can resist its temptations only with the help of the church. We should not imagine our children are free to make their own choice in the matter of discipleship any more than adults are. One way or another, all our lives reflect the choices that others have made for us, from our earliest days in the family home to the formational influences of the school room. We dare not leave our children undisciplined in the faith any more than we dare leave them undisciplined in what they eat or the clothes they wear. Whether baptized or dedicated, if our children are not raised with the discipline of Christian fellowship, we will be giving them up to the powers of worldliness. The question is, "Are we prepared to fulfill our vows as a whole community to be co-workers with God in this task of disciple making?"

In the next chapter, we will explore what it means to be baptized in both water and the Spirit. We will focus on how the gift of the Spirit is necessary for the church to live as a community of disciples on mission with God.

QUESTIONS FOR GROUP DISCUSSION

1. After reading this chapter, how have your views changed about the nature of Christian community and witness in the world?
2. To what extent does your church live under the shadow of Christendom? How could you become a more radical community of the kingdom?
3. What is the connection between holiness and mission? How does pursuing social holiness make us salt and light in the world?
4. Why are we warned against "friendship with the world"? How might this be reconciled with the idea of friendship evangelism?
5. Which parts of the fourfold pattern for remembering our baptism at the conclusion of this chapter do you find the most challenging? How is the Spirit guiding you?

CHAPTER 9

The Baptism of the Holy Spirit

Pour out your Holy Spirit, to bless this gift of water and those who receive it, to wash away their sin and clothe them in righteousness throughout their lives, that dying and being raised with Christ, they may share in his final victory."[1]

"Holy Spirit work within you, that being born through water and the Spirit, you may be a faithful disciple of Jesus.[2]

Remembering our baptism means seeking the gift of the Spirit for whole-life and lifelong discipleship. Are you being filled with the presence and power of the Spirit and living under his lordship as a holy witness in the world?

I n baptism, the use of water is an outward sign of the Spirit's gift of new life in Christ. Following baptism with water, there may also be laying on of hands with prayer to confirm the gift and work of the Spirit for empowering the onward journey of faithful discipleship.

Some have understood the work of the Spirit in baptism to mean that the rite actually causes us to be born again, especially in the case of infants. Others assume that new birth is a promise that waits to be fulfilled. I have no desire to enter that debate now! But in the baptism of converts, water is a sign that the new birth has already taken place, and this prayer is for the inward witness and empowerment of the Spirit for the life of discipleship. What remains unclear, however, is the connection between baptism with water and the promise that Jesus would baptize us with the Spirit.

In a hymn written especially for the baptism of adults, Charles Wesley wrote, "Sent to disciple all mankind, / Sent to baptize into thy name . . . Eternal Spirit, descend from high, / Baptizer of our spirits thou!"[3] There is a difference between confirming the work of the Spirit and praying for the baptism of the Spirit as a gift "from high." We have seen that the early Methodist movement was born in a time of revival with its emphasis on the gift of the Spirit as an inbreaking and life-changing experience. Indeed, there is a complex relationship between these aspects of the Wesleyan tradition and the emergence of the Pentecostal movement.[4] In this chapter, we will look at how their common roots in revival spirituality help us think about the connection between baptism in both water and the Spirit. In doing so, we will see how remembering our baptism enables us to reflect on the presence or absence of the Spirit's power in our lives.

Water and the Spirit

After Jesus had been baptized and rose up out of the water, the heavens opened and the Spirit came upon him in the form of a dove (Lk 4:21-22). John baptized Jesus with water as a sign of obedience to the Father, but the Father baptized Jesus with the Spirit as the power for his life and ministry. After the resurrection, Jesus instructed his disciples to wait in Jerusalem until they were "baptized in the Holy Spirit" and filled with power. This promise was fulfilled on the day of Pentecost when a bunch of fearful disciples were turned into bold witnesses for the gospel. The apostles then baptized others in the name of Jesus for the forgiveness of sins and prayed they would receive the gift of the Spirit as well. On their travels, they occasionally came across disciples who had been baptized only in the name of Jesus and immediately prayed for the gift of the Spirit with the laying on of hands (Acts 1:4-8, 2:38, 8:14-17).

The story of Paul's conversion has both these aspects of baptism. After his dramatic encounter with the risen Jesus on the Damascus road, Ananias laid hands on him, and he received the gift of the Spirit. Interestingly, this happened before Paul was baptized with water (Acts 9:9-18, 10:47-48). Clearly, the order of events holds no special regard for the mission of God. What mattered to the apostles was that the disciples of Jesus were baptized in both water and the Spirit. Where one was lacking, it was a problem to be remedied. When Paul discovered the Ephesians had received only the baptism of John for the repentance of sins, "they were baptized into the name of the Lord Jesus," and when he placed his hands on them, "the Holy Spirit came" (Acts 19:1-6). Sadly, a great many churches today are dysfunctional because they have never experienced the full meaning of baptism or encountered the power of the Spirit. There is something deficient in our Christian experience, and we are dying because of it.

Separated at Birth

In the early church, baptism included laying on of hands for the gift of the Spirit. With the coming of Christendom and the advent of infant baptism, this practice was delayed until confirmation. But eventually, confirmation became simply a renewal of the commitments associated with water baptism. Even where believer's baptism is practiced today, the dimension of Spirit-baptism is frequently neglected. The issue is not whether we are baptized with water in the name of the Spirit, but whether we

are immersed in the presence and power of the Spirit as a defi-
nite experience and working relationship. This is a question of
mission-critical importance.

The Pentecostal and Charismatic movements in recent years
have done much to revive this missing dimension of the Christian life.[5] Typically, they think of *baptism in the Spirit* as a moment
when the gift is consciously received for the first time. Some call
it a "second blessing," which follows initial conversion to faith in
Christ. Most think about being *filled with the Spirit* as a repeated
experience and a normal part of the Christian life. What matters
is that baptism in the Spirit must be actively sought if the gift has
not been received, and fullness of the Spirit should be the normal
expectation of all real Christians.

The Meaning of Pentecost

The Jewish festival of Pentecost, which comes fifty days after Passover, celebrates how God gave the Ten Commandments to Moses
on Mount Sinai, so the people might live in covenant relationship
with him and one another. The presence of God on the mountain
was manifest in thunder and lightening, blazing fire and clouds of
smoke, and the Israelites remembered this dramatic event every
year as a way of renewing their covenant with God.[6]

It is significant that the gift of the Spirit was poured out on
the day of Pentecost. The disciples were gathered in Jerusalem, on
Mount Zion, when the Spirit came in wind and fire. At the first
Pentecost, God established his covenant through the gift of law,
written on tablets of stone. On this new Pentecost, God renewed
the covenant by fulfilling the promises made to Ezekiel and Jer-
emiah that his law would be written on our hearts (2 Cor 3:3).
The meaning of Pentecost, then and now, is to form a holy people
who are empowered to live as witnesses to the kingdom of God.

The Outcome of Pentecost

Pentecost was a dramatic event. But when the rushing wind and tongues of fire died down, it was the abiding realities that mattered the most.

First, the gift of the Spirit led to a new boldness in witness, a new confidence in the gospel, a new freedom from fear, a new passion for the kingdom, and a new zeal for evangelism. Fifty days earlier, Peter had denied that he even knew Jesus and hid in an upper room, along with the other disciples, for fear of his life (John 20:19). But now, he stood before thousands and preached the greatest sermon of all time. This is what Jesus promised, "You will receive power when the Holy Spirit comes on you; and you will be my witnesses in Jerusalem, and in all Judea and Samaria, and to the ends of the earth" (Acts 1:8). The great Irish revivalist, William Arthur (1819–1901) argued that the "tongue of fire" is given to consume our hearts, drive out our fear, open our mouths, and anoint our speech with the power of the Spirit for witness in every area of life.[7]

Second, this gift and witness gave birth to the church, a new community of disciples who would fulfill the vocation of Israel to be "a light for the gentiles," and through whom "salvation may reach to the ends of the earth" (Is 49:6). This water-baptized and Spirit-filled community was empowered to fulfill the manifesto of Jesus laid out in the Beatitudes and the Sermon on the Mount. As a consequence, "the Lord added to their number daily those who were being saved" (Acts 2:46-47). Paul said we are all "baptized by one Spirit into one body" (1 Cor 12:13), because it takes the baptism and fullness of the Spirit to create a disciple-making community that shares in the mission of Jesus.

Third, the drama of Pentecost may have attracted a lot of attention, but it was the attractive witness of transformed lives that made a lasting impact on the world. We are baptized into a new and deeper working relationship with the Spirit that takes shape in a life of radical discipleship. There is a danger of spiritual idolatry if we seek the drama without the discipleship. But we are also in danger of power failure if we settle for less.

Fullness of the Spirit is promised to everyone. It is not some form of advanced discipleship but the normal Christian life.[8] The Spirit who descends upon us in tongues of flame also resides within us as fire in the heart. Our relationship with the Spirit is not like some torrid love affair of fleeting encounters with an exotic stranger. The Spirit comes to take up permanent residence in our hearts as a life-transforming power within and among us.

The Gift of the Spirit

Baptism in the Spirit should be an expectation, especially for new converts, and prayed for as part of their incorporation into the church. But what are we to do with those who are already baptized and members of the church who have never received the Pentecostal gift? Sadly, there is a widespread and multigenerational amnesia about what constitutes a fully baptized way of life, and the church ends up with the "form of godliness but denying its power" (2 Tim 3:5). In the shadow of Christendom, we are left striving to conform our lives to kingdom values without the life-transforming power of the Spirit in our hearts. This mindset leaves us powerless to resist the secularizing forces of our post-Christendom culture and without a credible witness to real Christian discipleship.

The opposite of normal Christianity is nominal Christianity. In the early Methodist movement, nominal Christians sought baptism in the Spirit as an experience of salvation they had never known before. The experience of Pentecost provided an abiding witness of the Spirit that they were children of the living God. There was an inexpressible joy, an incomprehensible peace, and an overwhelming love that filled their hearts and mouths with praise.

It was the experience of entering into a new realm of discipleship and a new depth of fellowship that was truly alive to God. There was a new hope, a new boldness to speak, and a new zeal to live and die for the sake of the gospel.[9]

The Wesleyan tradition has also maintained that if we have not experienced baptism in the Spirit, it does not mean the Spirit is absent from our lives. We only ever come to the Father through Jesus, and the work of his Spirit in conviction, repentance, and faith. Yet it is the great privilege of all real Christians to have a conscious relationship with the presence and the power of the Spirit, who vitalizes every aspect of our discipleship.[10] The true witness of baptism in the Spirit is not some prescribed form of spiritual experience but the visible transformation of our lives into the likeness of Jesus.

Baptism in the Spirit means coming into a fully personal, conscious and life-giving relationship with the triune God. The Spirit of adoption draws us into the same kind of relationship with God that Jesus enjoyed and causes our hearts to cry out "Abba! Father" (Rom 8:15). Then, the same Spirit of holiness renews our minds and conforms our lives to the likeness of his Son from the inside out. If this is missing, we need to pray for it!

The Fullness of the Spirit

Scripture also makes room for repeated encounters with the Spirit that renew the experience of Pentecost.[11] One such example comes a little later in Acts when the young church was faced with serious persecution and was beginning to lose its missionary nerve. After praying, "the place where they were meeting was shaken" and "they were all filled with the Holy Spirit and spoke the word of God boldly" (Acts 4:29-31). When Paul instructed the Ephesians to "be filled with the Spirit," it was in the present continuous tense. In other words, "keep on being filled" and don't let your spiritual lives run dry. This is normal discipleship, not some optional extra or deluxe edition of the Christian life. There is nothing the powers of worldliness like more than nominal Christians and spiritually anemic believers. Being filled with the Spirit is not merely a dramatic encounter or even a multiplicity of dramatic moments. To be filled continually means having the power to live as radical followers of Jesus and as witnesses for his kingdom in the moment-by-moment realities of everyday life.

REVIVAL SPIRITUALITY

The early Methodist movement was born in the soil of a great trans-Atlantic revival that swept across Britain, Ireland, America, and beyond. Revivals share the hallmarks of Pentecost in rebooting the mission of God through the church. The need for revival may or may not be associated with a decline in spiritual vitality, but it is always for the purpose of evangelism and making disciples.

A Definition of Revival

Andrew Walker and Kristin Aune define revivals as "movements of enthusiasm."[12] This is an apt description of the people called Methodists. In the eighteenth century, "enthusiasm" was a term of derision generally applied to those who claimed direct experience of the Spirit. The early Methodist movement intentionally promoted such personal experience, and it proved to be highly contagious. For Wesley, it was not the noise and drama of revival that fulfilled our Great Commission to spread the gospel throughout the earth. It was the flame of love that revival kindled in the heart, burning brightly through the transformed lives and passionate witness of ordinary Christians. So, he observed, "In general, it seems, the kingdom of God . . . will silently increase, wherever it is set up, and spread from heart to heart, from house to house, from town to town."[13]

Revival is a slippery idea to pin down, but most scholars seem to agree on a number of features. First, revival begins with those who long to see the flame of love rekindled in their own hearts, and it spreads from them to lukewarm believers in languishing churches. Second, the authenticity of revival is demonstrated in missionary zeal, leading to the conversion of both nominal Christians and unchurched people. Third, this process happens over an extended period of time and can spread from the neighborhood of a local church to an entire nation. If an encounter with the Spirit is confined to an individual disciple or community of disciples, it is more properly called "renewal" than revival. When the effects spread across a nation, however, they have been called "awakenings." The eighteenth century revival is often referred to as the "First Great Awakening," and the Methodist movement would certainly embody all three points.[14]

Remembering Our First Love

The meaning of revival can also be found in the psalmist's prayer, "Will you not revive us again, that your people may rejoice in you? Show us your unfailing love, O Lord, and grant us your salvation" (Ps 85:6-7). This weaves together the themes of revival, covenant renewal, and the way of salvation around the centrality of love. From this perspective, revival spirituality empowers us to face the powers of worldliness that threaten to rob us of our love for God, dampen our passion for holiness, and derail us from the journey of discipleship. Seasons and stories of revival are a reminder that the only way to break the power of sin and reignite a passion for holiness is through an encounter with the Spirit that renews our "first love."[15]

We see this principle worked out in the church at Ephesus (Eph 1:1-14). When Paul laid hands on them, the Spirit came in power. Later, he wrote to them from prison, celebrating how they had been chosen, forgiven, and adopted into the family of heaven, for a life of holy witness. All this was made possible through the "seal" of the Spirit, which empowered them for the journey of discipleship and enabled them to persevere against the odds. Paul cannot say often enough that all this was "to the praise of his glory."

When we get to the book of Revelation, however, the Spirit of Jesus has some comforting and disturbing words for the Ephesian church (Rev 2:1-7). They had been under considerable persecution, and Jesus first commends them for their endurance in the faith. They held fast to the truth of the gospel despite much suffering, even to the point of death. But doing the right stuff and condemning wickedness is not the nature of authentic witness. Equally, believing the right stuff and even being prepared to die for it was not the goal of their discipleship.

Jesus said, "I hold this against you: you have forsaken the love you had at first. Consider how far you have fallen! Repent and do the things you did at first." He warns them, "If you do not repent, I will come to you and remove your lampstand from its place" (Rev 2:4-5). If you do not remember your baptism, by turning back to God and seeking fresh oil for your lamp, your light will eventually die out. You will be worse than useless, a counter-witness to the kingdom, and must be taken out of the way. The witness of a Spirit-filled life is "sonship," not servility; joyful obedience, not slavish duty; and life-giving truth, not dead orthodoxy. Paul's prayer for the Ephesians makes it clear that love is not a sentiment but a power for holy living that comes from the indwelling Spirit of Christ, so that we may be "filled to the measure of all the fullness of God" (Eph 3:14-21).

The Methodist Pentecost

The early Methodists spoke of real Christianity as a religion of the heart, and the "fullness of God" came to be associated with the gift of perfection in love. In the early days of the revival, Charles Wesley said to his brother John, "Your day of Pentecost is not fully come, but I doubt not that it will; and you will then hear of persons sanctified, as frequently as you do now hear persons justified." These words were dramatically fulfilled in a season that has been called the "Methodist Pentecost" (1758–1763).[16] Looking back, John Wesley wrote, "the peculiar work of this season has been what Paul calls 'the perfecting of the saints' . . . They have been so filled with faith and love (and generally in a moment), that sin vanished . . . and they could rejoice evermore, pray without ceasing, and in everything give thanks."[17] As we have seen, Wesley defined perfection as "the humble, gentle, patient love of God and our neighbour, ruling our tempers, words, and actions."[18]

The need for this experience was felt most keenly by the early Methodist preachers, not merely for the sake of personal renewal but as the power for missionary service. Far from inducing a sense of pride, the experience of perfection was one of utter moment-by-moment dependence on God's grace and gifts.[19] Although many of the preachers were reluctant to speak of perfection as sinlessness, they enthusiastically talked about being "emptied of sin" in order to be "filled with love." For example, Jasper Robinson reflected that "contrary to my former expectation of being something extraordinary when sanctified, I am emptied of self, and sink into an unfeigned nothingness, that Christ may be my all in all."[20] Jane Cooper wrote in her journal, "My prayer has been for these fourteen years past that I may be nothing. And I praise God, I have reason to hope, that I come a little nearer to that blessed mark. I well know there is no happiness like that which flows from a constant sense that I am nothing and Jesus is all."[21] This is what it means to be baptized in the Spirit of Jesus.

SPIRIT-FILLED COMMUNITY

Paul instructed the Ephesians to "be filled with the Spirit" and "speak to one another with psalms, hymns and spiritual songs" (Eph 5.18-19). Singing hymns and spiritual conversation were regular features of early Methodist gatherings, from preaching services to the small-group meetings of classes and bands. Spirit-filled worship and the discipline of Christian fellowship went hand in hand on the journey of discipleship.

Society Meeting

Revival meetings could be wildly noisy or wonderfully solemn! A year in the life of a Methodist society might commence by renewing their covenant with God and end with a "watch-night" of fasting and prayer. Wesley observed that covenant services were occasions when "the windows of heaven were open," when God "did appear in the midst of the congregation," and when "the Spirit of glory . . . as usual, rested upon them." In the presence of God and filled with the Spirit, they freely surrendered their lives to Jesus.[22]

A hymn for the society meeting captures the charismatic nature of real Christian fellowship: "See, Jesu, thy disciples see, / The promised blessing give! / Met in thy name, we look to thee, / Expecting to receive." They gathered as the first disciples did in the upper room on the evening of Easter day, and prayed, "Breathe on us, Lord, in this our day, / And these dry bones shall live; / Speak peace into our hearts, and say, / 'The Holy Ghost receive!'"[23]

Singing Hymns

"Above all," Wesley said, "sing spiritually."[24] What matters more than the "spirit of poetry" in any hymn, is the "spirit of piety" with which it is sung. Hymns are a means of "kindling and increasing his love to God and man."[25] In the hymns for the society meeting, this piety was an expression of hearts that longed for more of God: "Come, Holy Ghost, all-quick'ning fire, / Come, and in me delight to rest! / Drawn by the lure of strong desire, / O come, and consecrate my breast." The Spirit is "lured" from above, by hearts that hunger and thirst for the holy life. "Eager for thee I ask and pant, / So strong the principle divine / Carries me out with sweet constraint, / Till all my hallowed soul is thine; / Plunged in the Godhead's deepest sea, / And lost in thy immensity."[26] Here is an allusion to baptism, and being "plunged" into the life of God, through water and the Spirit.

Baptized and born-again believers must fan the flame of the Spirit and keep pressing on to full salvation: "Come, Holy Ghost, my heart inspire! / Attest that I am born again! / Come, and baptize me now with fire, / Nor let thy former gifts be vain. / I cannot rest in sins forgiven; / Where is the earnest of my heaven?"[27]

Spiritual Friendship

The prayerful fellowship of class and band meetings was a means of grace for drawing close to Jesus and receiving the gift of his Spirit: "Jesu, united by thy grace, / And each to each endeared, / With confidence we seek thy face, / And know our prayer is heard." They were a "band of love, a threefold cord," sharing life intimately with one another and with the triune God: "Make us into one Spirit drink, / Baptize into thy name, / And let us always kindly think, / And sweetly speak the same." Here is a theology of charismatic fellowship in one simple stanza: "Touched by the loadstone of thy love, / Let all our hearts agree, / And ever towards each other move, / And ever move towards thee." The beauty of spiritual friendship is that the closer our fellowship with one another, the deeper is our communion with God.

One of the great privileges of belonging to such fellowship was the "love feast," which was a practice of the early church that Wesley discovered among the Moravians. The love feast was a time of shared testimony, where people of every age, sex, and walk of life could sing and speak of God's grace. On these occasions, Wesley often noted how "God poured out his Spirit abundantly" and how "the power of God fell upon all that were present."[28] These festivals of divine love were filled with shouts of praise, tears of joy, and fervent prayer. Many experienced the forgiveness of sins, deliverance from fear, comfort for grief, and the increase of faith. Others found the power of holy love could set their hearts free from the grip of worldliness and sin. And Wesley noted how "the flame ran from heart to heart," as the testimony of one ordinary person became a promise of God's grace to another.

Charles Wesley put it this way: "Jesu, we thy promise claim, / We are met in thy great name; / In the midst do thou appear, / Manifest thy presence here! / Sanctify us, Lord, and bless! / Breathe thy Spirit, give thy peace; / Thou thyself within us move, / Make our feast a feast of love."[29]

Stirring Hope

Wesley was unwavering in his defense of perfect love as an instantaneous gift of the Spirit, promised to all those who truly longed for holiness of heart and life. He advised his preachers that "constant experience shows, the more earnestly they expect this, the more swiftly and steadily does the gradual work of God go on in their soul . . . Whereas, just the contrary effects are observed whenever this expectation ceases."[30] He said, "they are 'saved by hope' by this hope of a total change, with a gradually increasing salvation. Destroy this hope, and that salvation stands still, or, rather, decreases daily." A central task of spiritual leadership from preaching services to small groups was to cast this vision of perfect love and encourage seekers to pursue it with all their heart. In the meantime, our constant prayer is, "Come, Holy Spirit!"

A letter from Hester Ann Roe to Ann Loxdale captures this stirring of hope quite beautifully:

> "Great things, indeed, my dear sister, has the Lord done for you . . . And yet, O stupendous grace! We have only received a drop from the ocean of his love. An endless prospect, and a maze of bliss, lie yet before us! Opening beauties, and such lengths, and breadths, and depths, and heights, as thought cannot reach or the mind of man conceive! It is, my friend, the fullness of the triune God, in which we may bathe, and plunge, and sink, till lost and swallowed up in the ever-increasing, overflowing ocean of delights. His fullness."[31]

This is what it means to be baptized and filled with the Spirit.

THE WAY TO PENTECOST

The hallmarks of revival spirituality include a hunger for God, renewal of spiritual discipline, serious repentance, openness to the Spirit, and a solemn dedication to follow Jesus in holiness of heart and life. The events of Pentecost remind us, however, that baptism in the Spirit is a sheer gift of grace poured out in God's own timing and must be received simply by faith when it comes. This raises the question: "Can we do anything to seek the gift of the Spirit, and promote revival?" From a Wesleyan perspective the answer is a cautious, "Yes."

Waiting for the Spirit

Just before his ascension, the risen Jesus told his disciples, "Wait in the city until you have been clothed with power from on high" (Lk 24:49, 52; also Acts 1:7-8). Their response was to wait at the Temple in Jerusalem by continually praising God. Yet when the Spirit came, it was not in the Temple but the upper room of the house where they were staying. Being of one heart and with one thing on their minds, "they all joined together constantly in prayer," and they were "all together in one place" when the promise was fulfilled (Acts 1:13-14, 2:1, 4:31). Clearly, "waiting" did not imply just standing still or getting on with business as usual. Rather, it meant exercising faith by adopting a posture of receptivity, with the expectation that the promise would be fulfilled (Lk 11:5-13).

Wesley taught the early Methodists that prayer was a "means of grace." In other words, it is a practice in which God has promised to meet us through the presence of his Spirit. The means of grace have no merit before God or power in themselves, but they are practices by which we stretch out empty hands of faith to receive the riches of his grace.[32] It is hard to exaggerate the importance of earnest prayer in stories of revival. From cottage meetings in England to frontier camp meetings in America, people assembled to seek revival through a combination of expectant prayer, impassioned singing, and spiritual conversation.

The Danger of Revivalism

In the nineteenth century, these organic means of grace were systematized into techniques for promoting revival and gave rise to the tradition of "revivalism." Charles Finney (1792–1875) developed a method for revival meetings that moved from impassioned singing to evangelical preaching and concluded with an altar call. This method was also adapted into "protracted meetings," which could last for several days of intense preaching, prayer, and singing. Holding revivals became an annual event in many churches and campgrounds across America, giving rise to professional revivalists and itinerating evangelists. In the twentieth century, revivalism evolved into the phenomenon of mass evangelism, exemplified by such household names as Billy Graham.

Notwithstanding the way God may have blessed these methods, there are a number of dangers with revivalism.[33] On the one hand, the aim was more focused on producing converts than making Spirit-filled disciples. Charles Finney claimed that revival "is not a miracle," merely "the result of the right use of the constituted means."[34] So, the means of grace were turned into the machinery of conversion. On the other hand, the legacy of revivalism has been dying churches that need constant re-evangelizing to keep their institutions going. For all these reasons, it is important to maintain a distinction between the gift of the Spirit in revival and the technological mindset of revivalism. Radical renewal is more likely to come from counting the cost of making disciples than funding more programs of church revitalization.

The Holiness Movement

Wesley taught the early Methodists to expect a gradual growth in grace and holiness through a commitment to the *General Rules* of society and the disciplines of Christian fellowship. But they also encountered the Spirit as an inbreaking, converting, and revolutionary power that changed their hearts and lives in a moment. So, they would wait on God in prayer and wrestle with him together for the instantaneous gift of new birth and the fullness of perfection in love.

Wesley's right hand man, John Fletcher, was the first to popularize the connection between the gift of Christian perfection and baptism in the Spirit. Hester Ann Rogers helpfully recounts an

encounter with Fletcher in which he explained how the gift of
"prophecy" promised by Joel and fulfilled at Pentecost (Acts 2:17)
would be given to everyone "renewed in love." He explained, "To
prophesy . . . was to magnify God with the new heart of love, and
the new tongue of praise, as they did, who, on the day of Pentecost, were filled with the Holy Ghost!" Rogers noted how Fletcher
"insisted that believers are now called to make the same confession, seeing we may all prove the same baptismal fire, showing
that the day of Pentecost was only the opening of the dispensation
of the Holy Ghost, the great promise of the Father!" Then, after a
hymn, he cried, "O to be filled with the Holy Ghost! I want to be
filled O my friends. Let us wrestle for a more abundant outpouring
of the Spirit."[35]

But do we need the gradual pursuit of holiness to have this
instantaneous gift of the Spirit? Phoebe Palmer (1807–1874),
mother of the "holiness movement," encouraged people to seek
the gift of perfect love by simply throwing themselves on the
altar in an act of total consecration to Jesus and his work. Palmer
called this the "shorter way" to receive the "second blessing."[36]
What Finney did for the process of conversion, Palmer did for
the pursuit of Christian perfection. Entire sanctification was not
something to wait for, but a gift to be claimed through faith. This
approach gave birth to various movements of enthusiasm with a
renewed commitment to evangelism and social action. Following
the theology of John Fletcher, these movements associated the
gift of entire sanctification with the baptism of the Spirit, which
was experienced as freedom from the tyranny of sin and empowerment for mission.

On the one hand, Wesley maintained that perfection in love
was a gift of the Spirit, and bestowed in a moment to those who
waited for it in the disciplines of discipleship. On the other hand,
the later holiness movement claimed the instantaneous gift of

spiritual power but stripped of the need for gradual growth in grace. Wesley himself did not confine baptism in the Spirit to the experience of perfect love because he wanted to avoid the conclusion that the Spirit was not given in power at the new birth. Nevertheless, the holiness movement brought the experience of revival to a later generation of Methodists, who had been born and baptized into a movement-turned-church with declining vitality. Perhaps this describes the situation of many churches today, and it is time to seek the gift of the Spirit again in new movements of enthusiasm.

Marks of True Revival

Jonathan Edwards was the great theologian of revival in the eighteenth century, and John Wesley republished versions of his work for the Methodist movement. Edwards argued that revival was merely an intensification of the ordinary work of the Spirit and should not be evaluated on the basis of extraordinary phenomena, although there were many. So, what is the ordinary work of the Spirit?

Edwards provided five criteria to evaluate true revival and the character of any movement of enthusiasm. He based them on 1 John 4, which invites us to "test the spirits" and "recognize the Spirit of God" in the church (4:1-2).[37] First, Jesus is worshiped as Savior and obeyed as Lord in the life of his disciples (4:2-3). Second, the Spirit brings conviction of sin and a longing for holiness (4:4-5). Third, true revival raises our esteem for the Bible and the pursuit of scriptural Christianity (4:6). Fourth, there is a renewed love for Scripture as the very word of God, a means of truth and grace for the journey of discipleship (4:6). Fifth, there is an increase in holy love for God and neighbor, expressed in works of piety and mercy and its overflow in mission (4:7-15).

REMEMBERING OUR BAPTISM

The baptism of the Spirit brings about a revolution in the soul. We are no longer to live as though life revolves around us, expecting God to bless our own wants and desires, either as individuals or the church. A fully baptized follower of Jesus knows that we do not possess God, but that his Spirit possesses, fills, convicts, and guides us. Remembering our baptism, then, presses us to ask: "Do we really want to be filled with the Spirit?"[38]

- **Initiation into the journey of discipleship.** The Spirit will insist that we deny ourselves and live in complete obedience to Jesus. But are we willing to surrender control of our lives and place them in the hands of God? Discipleship means no longer living for self but for the sake of his kingdom. It means discovering that we do not have what it takes for the journey in ourselves, but that we have all things when the Spirit is at work within and among us.

- **Dedication to the pursuit of holiness.** The Spirit will not allow us to flirt with temptation, or wink at perversity, or be indifferent to the things that God hates. He will insist that we set our minds on what Jesus desires, taking his teachings as our rule of life. But do we desire to have our lives conformed to Jesus? Are we willing to carry our cross and be set in opposition to the world? For the Spirit will not allow us simply to do what comes naturally any more or to follow what the world calls common sense. He will insist that we go the way of the cross, embrace a life of service, and perhaps even be hated by the world for it.

- **Participation in the mission of God.** The real proof of the Spirit-filled life does not lie in spiritual experiences, spectacular gifts, or special moments of grace. It is in the abiding reality of faithful hearts and obedient lives being made holy, set apart, and sent out as passionate witnesses to the kingdom of God. But do we really desire the Spirit's fire in our heart and his lordship over our lives? Are we willing to renew our covenant with God and truly place our lives at his pleasure and disposal? This is the kind of real Christianity, ablaze with love for God and neighbor, that might enable a post-Christendom world to catch the truth of the gospel for themselves.

- **Collaboration in disciple-making fellowship**. We may crave dramatic encounters with the Spirit in which we are swept away by the immensity of God's love, joy, and peace. We may covet the spectacular gifts of the Spirit, such as speaking in tongues, healing, and prophesy. We may even cherish the freedom and ecstasy of Spirit-filled worship, prayer, and praise. But do we really desire to be possessed by a spirit other than our own? Are we ready to give up our lives to God through committing ourselves to the discipline of Christian fellowship? We do not want to be counted among those who "trampled the Son of God underfoot" and "insulted the Spirit of grace" (Heb 10:29).

In the last chapter, we will draw together all the threads that have emerged throughout this book and offer some practical wisdom for how to remember our baptism and renew the church as a movement of enthusiasm in our day.

QUESTIONS FOR GROUP DISCUSSION

1. After reading this chapter, how have your views changed about baptism and fullness of the Spirit?
2. How does your church celebrate the gift of Pentecost and encourage people to be filled with the Spirit? Does this play a part in your services of baptism and confirmation?

3. Why is fullness of the Spirit so crucial for the life of discipleship? What does it mean to speak of the Spirit-filled life as normal Christianity?

4. What difference does it make to think of the Spirit filling
   the church, and not just individuals? What might be done to
   seek the baptism and fullness of the Spirit as a community of
   disciples?

5. Which parts of the fourfold pattern for remembering our baptism at the conclusion of this chapter do you find the most
   challenging? How is the Spirit guiding you?

CHAPTER 10

The DNA of a
Discipleship Movement

I am not afraid that the people called Methodists should ever cease to exist either in Europe or America. But I am afraid that it should only exist as a dead sect, having the form of religion without the power. And this undoubtedly will be the case unless they hold fast both the doctrine, spirit, and discipline with which they first set out (John Wesley).[1]

Remembering our baptism means belonging to the movement of Jesus, as Spirit-filled people on mission with God in the world. Are we thriving in the movement of God's love or merely going through the motions of church?

John Wesley bequeathed the Methodist movement with a cautionary prognosis about its future. If they forgot the reasons why God raised them up and failed to look for the power of his Spirit among them, they would only survive as a dead sect. There is a growing conviction that Wesley's prognosis should now be read as a diagnosis of contemporary Methodism and that revitalization of the church will depend on recovering its character as a disciple-ship movement.[2]

This book has been an exercise in holding on to the doctrine, spirit, and discipline of the early Methodist movement through the practice of remembering our baptism. Our approach has been particularly useful because it has pressed us to look back on the spiritual vitality of a movement from the standpoint of tepid denominationalism. In this concluding chapter, we will draw upon the biological metaphor of DNA as a way of identify-ing the "genetic code" or essential traits of early Methodism as a movement.

From the perspective of a discipleship movement, baptism is not about identification with any church tradition. We are not bap-tized as Methodists or in the name of any other denomination, but as followers of Jesus. Nevertheless, we are always baptized as children of God by incorporation into a household of faith, and our discipleship is inevitably expressed with certain family traits. So, our task will be to remember our baptism as an immersion in the Wesleyan "gene pool."

IMMERSION IN THE WESLEYAN "GENE POOL"

The church is first and foremost a community of disciples, and the revitalization of our churches will depend upon the renewal of authentic discipleship. The practice of remembering our baptism has enabled us to see the inseparable connection between disciple-ship and mission. Our first task is to restate the four ways this connection has been made in order to map the Wesleyan genome.[3] Then we will use that map to think through some practical impli-cations for local churches and church leadership.

Mapping the Genome of a Movement

We will start by remembering our baptism as a way of life that we each develop as followers of Jesus. This way of life can be described with four genetic traits that correlate to the fourfold pattern of remembrance we have used throughout the book:

- The first gene is **initiation into the life of discipleship**. Baptism is not just a mark of conversion or church membership. It is about becoming a lifelong and whole-life disciple of Jesus, which is marked by seeking growth in the holy love of God and neighbor.
- The second gene is **dedication to the pursuit of holiness**. Baptism is about growing in the life of discipleship and being transformed into the likeness of Jesus by using the disciplines of piety and mercy as means of grace.
- The third gene is **participation in the mission of God**. Baptism is about sharing in the ministry of Jesus as a citizen and servant of the kingdom. This is accomplished through engaging mission in the form of everyday witness.
- The fourth gene is **collaboration in disciple-making fellowship**. Baptism is a way of life that cannot be undertaken alone. Presenting a credible witness to the kingdom and living under the reign of God means sharing fellowship as co-workers in the gospel.

One way to think about remembering our baptism is that it should be a practice of "gene therapy," causing us to identify where our genetic code has been damaged or repressed, with the goal of healing and committing to fresh expressions of discipleship in our contemporary situation.

Gene Therapy for Communities of Discipleship

Remembering our baptism as communities of discipleship will confront us with the possibility that our spiritual life is languishing because we have invested more in the form of religion than the power of godliness. To put it more bluntly, our institutionalized denominations have been more concerned about running (and growing) churches than making (and growing) disciples. Reflecting on the purpose of church structure, Wesley asked, "What is the end of all ecclesiastical order? Is it not to bring souls from the power of Satan to God, and to build them up in His fear and love. Order, then, is so far valuable as it answers these ends; and if it answers them not, it is nothing worth."[4] There is an inseparable connection between the form and power of religion, insofar as the form becomes a means for seeking the power, and the power has an opportunity to be expressed in relevant forms. Nevertheless, Wesley said, "I would observe every punctilio of order, except where the salvation of souls is at stake."[5]

Baptism reminds us that the way we "do church" is valuable only insofar as it functions as a means of grace through which we become co-workers with God in making disciples. Contrary to this, however, is the conventional wisdom that revising structures will lead to the renewal of discipleship and the revitalization of congregations. My suggestion is that re-expressing the Wesleyan genome will involve a reversal of this logic. The pioneers of early Methodism did not set out to plant churches that could make disciples, but to "plant the gospel" and make disciples who needed (and longed for) empowering community. A commitment to revitalizing discipleship will more naturally lead to the renewal of the church and its structures. If we invest disproportionately in the form of religion, we end up with power failure. If we invest extravagantly in the power of godliness, we are more likely to end up with disciple-making communities.

Gene Therapy for Disciple-Making Leadership

Remembering our baptism as disciple-making leaders means ensuring that those we baptize are incorporated into a community that will help them grow in discipleship and mission. Leadership in mainline denominations, however, has typically been driven by the need for maintaining structures rather than making disciples.[6] On the one hand, the need to preserve denominational structures has made managerial competence an indispensable quality. But merely fulfilling the demands of institutional bureaucracy is an exhaustive task. On the other hand, the desire to preserve flagging membership has often turned pastoral ministry into a mixture of personal therapy and palliative care. The radical demands of authentic discipleship and mission have been concealed; and, as a result, the pursuit of holiness has been traded for cheap grace. We have tended to settle for spiritually impoverished lives with an anemic sense of God's presence and little expectation of his power to transform. Even where churches have tried to be more missional, they can end up repeating the same mistakes in new ways. We manage outreach projects, relevant worship, and fresh expressions without addressing the underlying nominalism and practical atheism that plagues ordinary Christian life. Or we run membership courses and discipleship programs as quick fixes for renewing the church and trying to increase our confidence in the gospel.

Baptism reminds us that real Christianity as a way of life is more caught than taught. It starts on the ground with ordinary people, desperate for God, who will do whatever it takes to become truly Jesus-shaped and Spirit-filled Christians. It grows when people gather in small groups for the discipline of Christian fellowship, and it spreads as grace abounds from heart to heart, home to home, and church to church.[7] The spirit of a movement calls for leaders who have a greater passion for making disciples than managing programs. This kind of passion comes from leaders who are growing as disciples themselves and who delight in opportunities to mentor others in the way of Jesus.

GENE 1—BAPTISM AS INITIATION INTO THE LIFE OF DISCIPLESHIP

Why do the "People called Methodists" matter? What is it that makes them distinctive enough to be worth preserving? As we have seen, John Wesley claimed that God raised up the Methodist movement "to reform the nation, particularly the church, and to spread scriptural holiness over the land." Second, he believed that the doctrine of "Christian perfection" was "the grand *depositum* which God has lodged with the people called Methodists; and for the sake of propagating this chiefly He appeared to have raised it up." In short, God had set them apart, and sent them out, to invite all people into a journey of discipleship, marked by holiness of heart and life, with the goal of perfect love. For William Sangster, this is Methodism's "unfinished task," and for which it must be "born again."[8]

Seeking Growth in Holy Love

We remember our baptism by seeking growth in holy love and longing for more of God's life-transforming presence and power in our hearts. From the Anglican Pietists, Wesley learned that holiness was a heart fully devoted to God, expressed in a life of loving obedience to Jesus.[9] From the Continental Mystics, he learned that holiness was the fruit of an intimate and conscious communion with God that takes flesh in costly service to others.[10] From the Moravian evangelicals, he learned that the pursuit of holiness is by faith and grace alone, begun in the experience of new birth and the personal assurance of forgiveness. And from the revivalists, he learned that this pursuit was empowered by the baptism and fullness of the Spirit. The gospel of early Methodism was an invitation to embark on a journey of discipleship in which the promise of evangelical conversion was a necessary step toward being saved to the uttermost.

Discipleship is a pursuit of holiness in which one is transformed into the likeness of Jesus through the power of the Spirit while "living on full stretch" for the gift of perfect love.[11] This pursuit is motivated by a longing for life to be made beautiful by the indwelling presence and power of God. The "beauty of holiness" is seen in the life of Jesus, and discipleship is about becoming more like him in all our thinking, feeling, speaking, and doing. When those who live without God come into contact with a people whose lives are radiant with divine beauty, the truth of the gospel is not only credible but also attractive and compelling.

Holy Living and Healthy Churches

We remember our baptism as a community of discipleship by making growth in grace our main business. But the Wesleyan gene of seeking holiness can be repressed by a preoccupation with restructuring the church. Viewed positively, the motivation for restructuring lies in negotiating the tension between a fear of diminishing resources and the hope for promoting renewal and mission activity. This leads to the development of mission statements, priorities, and core values to guide new ways of working. The generation of new structures also entails new leadership and committees to manage the new future. Scripture teaches us that you should not put new wine in old wineskins, but tradition suggests that you do not get new wine just by making new wineskins (see Lk 5:36-39).

Unfortunately, when we start with church structures, the structures typically become an end in themselves rather than a means of grace. Renewal easily gets confused with implementing some new vision of "doing church," and discipleship is reduced to serving the structures, all in the name of mission. If we start with discipleship, however, we are driven by a different question: "What kind of people do we want to be?" The gene of seeking holiness shapes a desire to become people who delight in the gospel of holy love and who seek the fullness of a Jesus-shaped and Spirit-filled life. This wisdom warns us that changing structures without the goal of changed lives will not lead to healthy churches. But those who long for more of God also long for structures that can help them become more faithful disciples. Adapt to meet that need and people will seek the spiritual life through which the church can be renewed.

Creating a Hunger for More of God

We remember our baptism as disciple-making leaders not just by feeding the flock but by making them hungry for more of God. One dominant image of church leadership has been the pastoral imperative to "feed the flock" so that they might feel satisfied and happy. Leaders rightly invest their resources in creating worship experiences to lift the spirit; or they lead study groups to inspire the mind; or they give care to comfort the soul. But when the church becomes satisfied with these activities as ends in themselves, it can actually inoculate people from sensing the need for deep and lasting spiritual growth. It must be remembered that Jesus also said, "blessed are those who hunger and thirst for righteousness, for they will be filled" (Mt 5:6).

Among the early Methodist preachers, John Nelson's antidote to apathy among the early Methodists was "to create such a hungering and thirsting in them after inward holiness . . . till all that is in them be made holiness to the Lord." In the midst of a powerful love feast, John Furz recalled how some local leaders were "so filled with zeal for the glory of God and the good of souls" that they "went into the country villages, sung and prayed, and exhorted people to turn to God." George Shadford reflected, "If we had more of God in our hearts, there would be more of him on our tongues and shining in our lives."[12]

The Wesleyan gene of seeking holiness reminds us that we were made for an intimate and daily sense of God's life-transforming presence and power. Making disciples who desire to grow means encouraging them to hunger for more of God in their own lives and for the kingdom of God in their communities. The spirit of a movement calls for leaders who long for the fullness of spiritual life in themselves and are committed to sharing these desires with others. After the manner of love feasts, disciple-making leaders will encourage people to share their longings and inspire one another with real-life testimonies of personal transformation and everyday mission.

GENE 2—BAPTISM AS DEDICATION TO THE PURSUIT OF HOLINESS

Once captivated by the promises of scriptural holiness, Wesley encouraged the early Methodists to strive for evangelical conversion and perfection in love by using the spiritual disciplines as means of grace.[13] By these means, we become co-workers in what Wesley called the two "grand branches" of salvation. On the one hand, grace is everything that God has done for us in Christ to forgive our sins and bring us into right relationship with the Father (i.e., justifying grace). On the other hand, grace is everything that God does in us through the Spirit to give us new birth, set us free from the power of sin, and conform our lives to the likeness of Christ (i.e., sanctifying grace). If it is by grace that God reaches out to embrace us, then it is by faith that we enter into that embrace. The means of grace are the practices in and through which this encounter with God takes place and transforms our lives.

Using Spiritual Disciplines as Means of Grace

We remember our baptism by seeking growth through the spiritual disciplines as a way of staying connected to God's grace. The spiritual disciplines are means of grace through which this life-transforming communion with God is entered, deepened, and extended. They are also the means by which we wait for the baptism and fullness of the Spirit. The means of grace can be grouped into works of piety and works of mercy.[14] In one sense, it might be said that the love of God is cultivated primarily through works of piety, and love of neighbor is expressed primarily through works of mercy. In another sense, however, they are inseparable because cultivating intimacy with God will inevitably send us out to meet the needs of others. When works of piety lead to works of mercy, we are caught up in a movement of divine grace that fills, transforms, and overflows our hearts and lives. Using these disciplines as means of grace is how we become recipients of, and participants in, the mission of God.

Wesley warned that we cannot make serving God in works of piety an excuse for neglecting our neighbor in works of mercy. If it comes to a choice, we must be ready to leave the sanctuaries of private devotion or public worship "at charity's almighty call."[15] This relationship between devotion and mission is perfectly embodied in the life of Jesus. In him, zeal for works of mercy was the immediate overflow of his intimate relationship with God in the power of the Spirit.

Spiritual Discipline and Authentic Worship

We remember our baptism as communities of discipleship by helping one another walk closely with God in everyday life. But the Wesleyan gene of spiritual discipline can be repressed by a preoccupation with worship services. In most congregations, the

Sunday service defines what it means to "do church." Discipleship amounts to attendance at worship, and mission is about attracting new churchgoers to improve our attendance records. The church strives to make its services lively, creative, and transforming. A lot of time is spent arguing about musical style, how messy worship can be, and whether people are satisfied. Behind all this, there is an unspoken assumption that God is more real, present, and active during one hour on a Sunday morning than in the 24/7 realities of everyday life. People will talk about attending church to "recharge their batteries" for the God-forsaken week that lies ahead. They arrive "flat," or half dead, hoping for a jump-start back to life. So, worship leaders try to oblige, while getting worn out and disillusioned in the process.

Unfortunately, when we start with church services, we are likely to end up as consumers rather than disciples. People attend a church service to binge on one good meal and then starve for the rest of the week. If we start with discipleship, however, we ask a different question: "What kind of worshipers do we want to be?" The gene of spiritual discipline shapes a desire to become people who practice the presence of God, pray without ceasing, and give thanks in all circumstances every day of the week. Wesley asked, "What is it to worship God? . . . It is, to love him, delight in him, to desire him with all our heart, and mind, and soul, and strength; to imitate him we love . . . to go through outward work with hearts lifted up to him; to make our daily employment a sacrifice to God."[16] This wisdom warns us that renovating church services without deepening our walk with God will not lead to authentic worship. For those who are immersed in the means of grace, worship services are not the start of a Godless week but the culmination of a God-filled week. Adapt to this way of life, and corporate worship provides an opportunity to celebrate the reality of God's presence and goodness through the ups and downs of daily life.

Equipping People for Intimacy with God

We remember our baptism as disciple-making leaders not just by doing ministry but by equipping people for practicing the presence of God in daily life. Church leaders spend much of their energy striving to help people encounter God on special occasions and at certain times of the week. They invest their resources in arranging prayer meetings, leading Bible studies, and conducting pastoral visits. The problem comes when this perpetuates the idea of an "omnicompetent" leader who insulates people from the personal responsibility of discipleship and the challenge of everyday mission. Jesus did not merely pray for his disciples, he taught them how to develop a relationship with God for themselves: "This, then, is how you should pray: 'Our Father . . . Give us this day. . . .'" (Mt 6:9).

The early Methodist preachers understood that intimacy with God was the life of discipleship and mission. Jonathan Maskew insisted that "a Christian can as well live without food, see without eyes, or walk without feet, as live to God without secret prayer." Furthermore, Thomas Walsh set an example of one who lived in "a momentary spirit of watchful prayer" whether "prostrate upon his face, kneeling, standing, walking, eating, in every posture, and in every place and condition."[17]

The Wesleyan gene of spiritual discipline reminds us that we were made to hear God's still small voice of guidance in the messy details of life, to see his presence in our neighborhoods, and to share his heart for the least and the lost. Equipping disciples for daily life means teaching people how to pray and practice the presence of God. The spirit of a movement calls for leaders who long for God's transforming presence and know how to help others stay connected with God's grace in all the spiritual disciplines.

GENE 3—BAPTISM AS PARTICIPATION IN THE MISSION OF GOD

As we have seen, seeking holiness and spiritual discipline contribute to a God-centered life that is missional by nature. Mission is best understood as the character of a holy people who are set apart for God and sent out into the world. Wesley affirmed that "the root of religion lies in the heart, in the inmost soul." But "if this root be really in the heart, it cannot but put forth branches" through our lives and into the world.[18]

Engaging Mission as Everyday Witness

Remembering our baptism means paying attention to the movements of the Spirit in daily life and surrendering to his lead in our words and deeds. We have seen that the ethos of everyday mission can be embodied in what Wesley called "social holiness." By this, he does not mean engagement in social activism or working for social justice as such. Rather, Wesley means that we are all situated in a nexus of personal relationships through which the life, love, and grace of God may be revealed and spread to others. It means living as the "salt of the earth" and as the "light of the world." Social holiness is the kind of incarnational life found in Jesus, which makes the gospel visible in our lives and relationships, as the church both gathered and scattered.

The spirit of everyday mission is also encapsulated in Wesley's principle of "good stewardship."[19] A good steward is one who knows that life is not given for us to do as we please, but to do what pleases God so that his kingdom purposes may be fulfilled through us. Life is a gift from God, not to be owned and possessed but to be enjoyed in the process of giving it back to God by serving

others in word and deed. All our intellectual powers, bodily capacities, material wealth, time, and talents are to be surrendered into
God's hands, moment-by-moment, as each occasion demands.
It required a sense of good stewardship and a missionary heart
for the early Methodists to engage the annual practice of renewing their covenant with God. But Wesley actually taught them to
remember their vows in the weekly prayer, "To thee, O God . . .
I give up myself entirely: May I no longer serve myself, but thee,
all the days of my life . . . Be thou the sole disposer and governor
of myself and all; be thou my portion and my all."[20] For Wesley,
good stewardship and prayerful surrender are embodied in a life
of social holiness, as God "sends" us to serve our families, friends,
neighbors, and strangers.

Perhaps the most strategic method commended by Wesley
was visiting the sick and needy. Although there is no formula for
this practice, he said, "It may not be amiss, usually, to begin with
inquiring into their outward condition" and bodily needs. Yet he
urged, "that you still keep a higher end in view, even the saving of souls from death, and that your labour to make all you say
and do subservient to that great end."[21] The general implication
of Wesley's thinking is that God "brings" others into our realm of
influence, on a daily basis, often in unexpected ways. We are never
short of opportunities to serve others in works of mercy; the only
question is whether we will surrender to the impulses of the Spirit
when they arise.

Everyday Witness and Effective Outreach

Remembering our baptism as a community of discipleship means
encouraging one another to abide deeply with God in order to live
missionally in the world. But the Wesleyan gene of everyday mission can be repressed by our propensity for mission projects and
programs when they become ends in themselves. The process is

familiar: Find a worthy cause; then delegate a mission commit-
tee; then develop an outreach strategy; then design a program of
events; and finally drum up volunteers to run them. A mission
strategy becomes an end in itself when we congratulate ourselves
on having a well-run program, even if it does not lead to making
new disciples. It is an open secret that people are evangelized by
faith-sharing relationships, not well-run programs, as such. Mission activities will be effective only if the Christians who participate are filled with the love of God and overflowing with love of
neighbor. People who are not alive to God have no life to share
with others. In short, true mission must flow from authentic
discipleship.

Let me be plain: Our strategies, projects, and programs can be
extremely valuable if they are developed to provide opportunities
for Christians to share their faith. But for that to happen, we must
be raising disciples who have good news to share and whose lives
have become missionary by nature. Unfortunately, when we start
with mission strategy, we can end up running programs rather
than sharing faith. If we start with discipleship, however, we ask
a different question: "What kind of witnesses do we want to be?"
The gene of everyday mission shapes a vision of becoming people
who are alive to God and share God's heart for others. We are to
become people who seize everyday opportunities to love others
in word and deed, openly sharing our faith one work of mercy
at a time. For Wesley, visiting the sick was a missional discipline
incumbent upon all Christians, and he believed that failure to
serve as the Spirit leads would cause our spiritual life to gradually
wither and die.[22] Self-centeredness not only cheats our neighbor
of what God intended, but it kills the very life of God in the soul.
On the one hand, this wisdom warns us that developing mission
strategies without making mission-shaped disciples will not lead
to effective outreach. On the other hand, those who are seeking
to abide deeply in God and live missionally in the world will see

our programs as opportunities for building relationships of witness and faith sharing. Adapt to this approach by raising disciples who are missionary by nature, and we will share the kind of faith that makes more disciples and renews the church.

Raising Missionaries as Co-Workers with God

Remembering our baptism as disciple-making leaders means that we don't just plan missions, we raise missionaries. Very often, church leaders think of engaging mission in terms of ambitious, high-risk, and creative activities. They organize evangelistic events, door-to-door visitation, seeker services, and church plants. Care must be taken, however, that commitment to this kind of activity does not blind us to the opportunities we have for sharing faith in the ordinary encounters of daily life. Jesus did not appear to have anything like what we would recognize as a mission strategy other than living as a co-worker with the Father by touching and transforming the lives of all he met. He saw the people around him as those to whom God was reaching out with his love. Jesus said, "Whatever the Father does the Son also does" for "it is the Father, living in me, who is doing his work" (Jn 5:19, 14:10).

As a young convert in the early Methodist movement, William Black recounted, "I felt a peculiar love to souls, and seldom passed a man, woman, or child without lifting up my heart to God on their account . . . so that sometimes I was constrained to speak to them, though I met with rough treatment in return."[23] In his ministry among the early Methodists, the zeal of Thomas Walsh was an example of stewardship and surrender, being resolved "to give himself up wholly to the dictates of the Holy Ghost, and to be ready to go what way soever the voice of heaven should call him." Having "a heart always at leisure for God, attentive to His teaching, and obedient to His dictates, is the great thing; to which every design and pursuit must give place, if we mean to be truly great in the grace of God."[24]

The Wesleyan gene of everyday mission reminds us that we are made with the ability to sense the impulses of the Spirit in the flow of daily life and surrender to these opportunities for serving others, one work of mercy at a time. The spirit of a movement calls for leaders who long to see God at work through their own lives and know how to help others become fully surrendered co-workers in the kingdom.

GENE 4—BAPTISM AS COLLABORATION IN DISCIPLE-MAKING FELLOWSHIP

Seeking holiness means striving for a God-centered life through the spiritual disciplines. It takes deep spiritual friendships of mutual accountability and spiritual guidance, however, to keep us attentive to God and intentional about the pursuit of discipleship and mission. Wesley taught the early Methodists that there was no such thing as "solitary Christianity," because he was convinced that the pursuit of holiness would fail apart from the support of spiritual friends who shared the journey of discipleship together.

Sharing Fellowship on the Journey of Discipleship

We remember our baptism by investing in the fellowship of spiritual friends for the journey of discipleship. The contemporary church can be quite intentional about worship and pastoral care while completely neglecting the need for mutual accountability and spiritual guidance. Yet this kind of spiritual conversation was the essence of early Methodist fellowship and the heartbeat of class and band meetings. People are right to be wary of accountability if it is associated with forms of evaluation, reward, and punishment,

rather than sharing, healing, and growth. But the small groups
in early Methodism had the goal of helping one another become
more attentive to the presence of God and more responsive to the
leading of the Spirit in their lives. The challenge of deep spiritual
friendship was grasped as a blessing, albeit with "fear and trembling," by those who longed to abide more deeply in God's grace
and live more fully into his purpose for their lives.

Spiritual Friendship and Real Community

We remember our baptism as communities of discipleship by
prioritizing the discipline of Christian fellowship. Ironically, the
Wesleyan gene of sharing fellowship can actually be repressed by
multiplying small groups. Growing numbers of churches are discovering the benefit of small groups for making deeper friendships
and growing in love for one another. Indeed, these groups can be
where we "do church" most meaningfully, especially when church
politics and Sunday services leave us cold and weary. One life-
giving feature of small groups is that they are organized around
hearing, reading, and studying the Scriptures. For an increasing
number of people, however, there is a growing suspicion that all
this fellowship still makes little impact on everyday life. So, we try
to increase the spiritual depth of our meetings by making them
more creative, interactive, and experiential. As a result, we may
find ourselves better informed, and even convicted, but still not
really changed.

Unfortunately, it seems as though we are caught on the horns
of a dilemma. On the one hand, if we start with the need for
friendship, we may end up with social circles rather than spiritual communities. On the other hand, by starting with the need to
study, we may become leaners about Jesus but not real followers
of Jesus. If we start with discipleship, however, we ask a different
question: "What kind of friends do we want to be?" The gene of

sharing fellowship shapes a vision of becoming people who hold one another accountable for our daily walk with God–people who help one another discern God's presence and follow God's lead in the flow of everyday life. This wisdom warns us that multiplying small groups without deepening spiritual friendships will not lead to real fellowship. But those who invest in deep spiritual conversation will be most stretched in both their love and service, as hearers and doers of the word. Adapt to this, and we will love one another, as well as live the gospel more faithfully.

Investing in a Few Who Share the Life of God

We remember our baptism as disciple-making leaders not just by attracting crowds but by investing in a few for the sake of the many. Many church leaders have been trained to think that making a difference means attracting a crowd and affecting as many people as possible through high-impact meetings. Ministry by mass appeal has not only influenced our worship gatherings and outreach activities but our discipleship strategies as well. We try to make disciples by delivering conferences, training events, courses, and workshops. When leaders are turned into experts rather than spiritual guides, however, they are absolved of the need to be "real" examples and mentors. Although Jesus did attract crowds, his main strategy for changing the world was to invest in a few for the sake of the many: "He appointed twelve that they might be with him and that he might send them out" (Mk 3:14). He invested in deep spiritual friendships with a small group of disciples and an even smaller "band" of three (Peter, James and John). Jesus shared his life with them in three years of intensive spiritual formation, so they might become like him and continue his mission.

Thomas Rankin celebrated how "the whole economy of Methodism" (i.e., societies, classes, and bands) worked together "to promote the great end for which they were designed—the glory of

God in the salvation of souls."[25] Taking on the responsibility for a class meeting was typically how leaders were raised up, and meeting in bands was how they sustained themselves through the challenges of ministry. Wesley established the "select bands" to invest personally in raising up leaders who would be "a pattern of love, of holiness, and of good works" for the movement.[26]

The Wesleyan gene of sharing fellowship reminds us that disciples are made through sharing life deeply with others in relationships of mutual accountability and spiritual guidance. The spirit of a movement calls for leaders who long for God's guidance themselves and know how to help others find it through deep spiritual conversation. Disciple-making leaders will do the work of spiritual guides by investing in a few at a time. Those few, in turn, become capable of multiplying that investment in the lives of many others. I recommend the ministry of Covenant Discipleship and the Inspire Movement as contemporary innovations on the Wesleyan class and band meetings.[27]

Conclusion

In his sermon, *On Zeal*, Wesley set out a model for discipleship based on an arrangement of concentric circles that nicely mirrors the genome outlined above.[28] The inner core of discipleship is the love of God and neighbor, rooted in the heart. Next to this are the inner desires and motivations, which are shaped by this holy love (Gene 1). Surrounding these character traits are the works of piety and mercy, through which the love of God is cultivated (Gene 2). Finally, the whole is encompassed by the fellowship of the church, which is both a means of grace and the visible witness of social holiness in the world (Genes 3 and 4).

Wesley defined zeal as a fervent and godly passion shaped by "the flame of love" for God and neighbor. He was clear that our zeal must work from the inside out; or, rather, it must increase

Inside-Out Discipleship
Adapted from John Wesley, Sermon, *On Zeal*

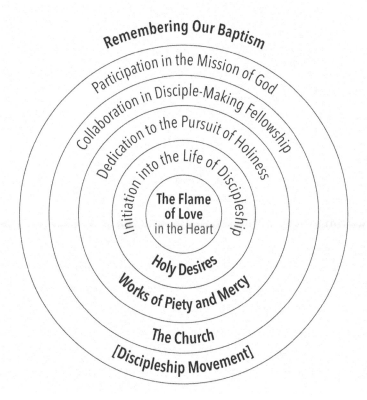

from the outside in! We must be zealous for the church and its structures and that the church should grow in both number and influence. But if this zeal is not directed by a zeal for the life and love of God in the soul, then doing church will become an end in itself instead of provoking its members to abound in love and good works. So, we must be more zealous for the works of piety and mercy than for the forms of church life. But if we become preoccupied with these means as ends in themselves, they can also become life-sapping and counterproductive. So, we must be more zealous still for the character that they are meant to form, and yet more zealous for the holy love that nourishes the whole.

For Wesley, this order of priority was meant to ensure that the life and love of God can expand from the heart through our inward character, shaped by the means of grace, disciplined by Christian fellowship, and then out into the world as the visible witness of holy lives. This is the pursuit of mission-shaped discipleship. This is what it means to remember our baptism.

Questions for Group Discussion

1. After reading this chapter, how have your views changed about the nature of discipleship and church renewal?
2. As you reflect on the spiritual vitality of your church, what are your reflections on Wesley's fears about Methodism becoming a "dead sect," having the form of religion without the power?
3. How do you respond to the central questions posed in this chapter: "What kind of disciple do you want to be? What kind of worshiper do you want to be? What kind of witness do you want to be? What kind of friend do you want to be?"
4. What is spiritual hunger? Why might it be the key to authentic discipleship and the renewal of the church? How could you encourage one another to be hungry for more of God, his way of life, and his reign in the world?
5. Which parts of the fourfold pattern for zeal at the conclusion of this chapter do you find the most challenging? How is the Spirit guiding you?

ENDNOTES

INTRODUCTION

1. The theme of remembering our baptism has been taken up by most church traditions: (1) In the Methodist tradition, see https://www.umc discipleship.org/resources/new-service-of-reaffirmation-of-the-baptismal -covenant; (2) In the Roman Catholic tradition, when celebrating the feast of the baptism of Jesus, see http://w2.vatican.va/content/francesco /en/audiences/2014/documents/papa-francesco_20140108_udienza -generale.html; (3) In the Mennonite tradition, see https://themennonite .org/feature/remembering-baptism-2; (4) In the Reformed tradition, see https://www.reformedworship.org/article/december-1989/remember -your-baptism; and http://worship.calvin.edu/resources/resource-library /remembering-baptism-living-wet/ (All accessed, June 2017).

2. See the study guide, *By Water and the Spirit: Making Connections for Identity and Ministry* by Gayle Carlton Felton (Discipleship Resources, 1997), chs.5, 6; and William Willimon, *Remember Who You Are: Baptism, a Model for Christian Life* (Upper Room, 1984).

3. See Paul Althaus, *The Theology of Martin Luther* (Fortress Press, 1966), chs.18, 26, and Gerhard O. Forde, *Where God Meets Man: Luther's Down-to-Earth Approach to the Gospel* (Augsburg Publishing House, 1972), ch. 5.

4. Dietrich Bonhoeffer, *The Cost of Discipleship* (SCM Press, 1959), 35.

5. See Theodore Runyon, *The New Creation: John Wesley's Theology for Today* (Abingdon Press, 1997), 140–145; Henry Knight, *The Presence of God in the Christian Life* (Scarecrow Press, 1992); Gayle Carlton Felton, *This Gift of Water* (Abingdon Press, 1992), chs.1, 2; Ole Borgen, *John Wesley on the Sacraments* (Francis Asbury Press, 1972); Bernard Holland, *Baptism in Early Methodism* (Epworth Press, 1970).

6. See Treatise. John Wesley adapted this from his father Samuel's pamphlet, *A Pious Communicant* (1716).

7. See Lawrence Mick, *Living Baptism Daily* (Liturgical Press, 2004).

8. See Kenneth Collins, *A Real Christian: The Life of John Wesley* (Abingdon Press, 2000).

9. Bonhoeffer, *The Cost of Discipleship*, 32.

CHAPTER ONE

1. Covenant, §10.

2. Notes, Mt 28:19.

3. *The Book of Discipline of the United Methodist Church* (United Methodist Publishing House, 2004), 87, ¶120.

4. *God's Mission, Our Mission* (Methodist Church in Ireland, 2014), 1, ¶1.4. Although it is not specifically connected to the Great Commission, the British Methodist Church has attempted to make discipleship the defining center of its identity, in *Contemporary Methodism: A Discipleship Movement Shaped for Mission* (The Methodist Church, 2011).

5. See A.B. Bruce, *The Training of the Twelve* (1871), and Robert Coleman, *The Master Plan of Evangelism* (Revell, 2006).

6. In John's Gospel, Jesus tells us that he only does what he sees the Father doing and says only what he hears the Father saying (Jn 5:30, 8:28). When viewed through the life of Jesus, we see that the principle of imitation is not merely copying the example of the Father but having the kind of life that flows from an intimate communion with him. Similarly, discipleship as the imitation of Jesus flows from our abiding in him and his Spirit abiding in us (14:25, 15:5). It is a life of moment-by-moment guidance, empowerment, and obedience.

7. Sermon, "The General Spread of the Gospel," ¶13–14, WJW 6.

8. In what follows, I am indebted to the work of Paul Hertig, "The Great Commission Revisited: The Role of God's Reign in Disciple Making," *Missiology: An International Review*, 29:3 (2001), 343–351; Jacques Matthey, "The Great Commission According to Matthew," *International Review of Mission*, (1980), 161–173; and Walter McConnell, "Discipleship and the Great Commission," *Mission Round Table*, 9:2 (2014), 12–17.

9. Mortimer Arias, "The Church in the World: Rethinking the Great Commission," *Theology Today*, 47:4 (1991), 411.

10. See William Abraham, *The Logic of Evangelism* (Eerdmans, 1996), and Scott Jones, *The Evangelistic Love of God and Neighbor* (Abingdon Press, 2003).

11. Dallas Willard, *The Divine Conspiracy* (Fount, 1998), ch. 9.

12. See Michael Green, *Evangelism in the Early Church* (Kingsway, 2003).

13. World Council of Churches (WCC), *Baptism, Eucharist and Ministry*, Faith and Order Paper 111 (1982), 1.

14. WCC, *Baptism*, 2.

15. The Alpha Course, developed by Holy Trinity, Brompton, an evangelical Anglican church in London, has become popular around the world. See http://alpha.org. For an explanation of the Alpha Course, see Philip Meadows, "The Alpha Course," in: Stephen Gunter and Elaine Robinson (Eds.), *Considering the Great Commission* (Abingdon Press, 2006).

16. Tom Hardwick, *Not Wasted* (Self Published, 2015). Available from Amazonathttps://www.amazon.co.uk/Not-Wasted-Tom-Hardwick-ebook /dp/B00TL03I90/ (Accessed, June, 2017).

Chapter Two

1. Covenant, §12–13.

2. John Stott, *Christian Mission in the Modern World* (IVP, 2008), 29–31.

3. Martin Klauber and Scott Manetsch, *The Great Commission: Evangelicals and the History of World Missions* (B&H Publishing, 2008), 1–9.

4. John Wesley (Ed.), *An Extract of the Life of the Late Rev. David Brainerd, Missionary to the Indians* (1768). This was an edited version of Jonathan Edwards, *Life of David Brainerd* (1735). See also John Grigg, *The Lives of David Brainerd* (Oxford, 2009), 148–163.

5. Minutes, 24.

6. See J.E. Hutton, *A History of Moravian Missions* (Moravian Publication Office, 1922). https://archive.org/details/historyofmoravia00huttuoft.

7. The Christian Library contains editions of Edwards's treatises, *A Faithful Narrative of the Surprising Work of God* (1735); *The Distinguishing Marks of a Work of the Spirit of God* (1758); *A Treatise Concerning Religious Affections* (1754).

8. Sermon, "The Catholic Spirit," §I.11, II.2, WJW 5.

9. Minutes, 13.

10. Minutes, 25.

11. Minutes, 33.

12. Minutes, 35.

13. Minutes, 30–31.

14. William Carey, *An Enquiry into the Obligations of Christians to Use Means for the Conversion of the Heathens* (1792). See, https://itun.es/gb /SiekE.l (Accessed, June 2017).

15. Carey, *Enquiry*, 118.

16. See Darrell Guder (Ed.), *Missional Church: A Vision for the Sending of the Church in North America* (Eerdmans, 1998). From a British perspective, see *Mission-Shaped Church* (Church House, 2004).

17. See Philip Meadows, "The DNA of Mission-Shaped Discipleship," in Joseph Cunningham (Ed.), *Contemporary Perspectives in Wesleyan Thought* (Emeth Press, 2013). Also Susan Hope, *Mission-Shaped Spirituality* (Church House: 2010); and Roger Helland & Leonard Hjalmarson, *Missional Spirituality* (IVP, 2011).

18. The full text can be found at http://www.methodist.org.uk/news -and-events/news-releases/"bring-one-person-to-faith-this-year" -methodist-president-urges-churches (Accessed, June 2016).

19. *The Constitutional Practice and Discipline of the Methodist Church*, 2 (2015), 213.

20. Dallas Willard, *The Great Omission: Reclaiming Jesus' Essential Teachings on Discipleship* (Monarch, 2006), x.

21. Willard, *Great Omission*, xiv. As noted more extensively in chapter 10, the problem for leadership is not the potential value of programs themselves, but the temptation toward programmatic forms of ministry that do not require much of our discipleship or disciple making.

22. Sermon, "The General Spread of the Gospel," WJW 6. Wesley takes the text from Is 11:9.

23. Sermon, "General Spread," ¶26–27. See Rev 7:12.

24. Sermon, "General Spread," ¶9.

25. Sermon, "General Spread," ¶17.

26. Sermon, "Scriptural Christianity," ¶7, WJW 5. See also Sermon, "The Causes of the Inefficacy of Christianity," WJW 7.

27. Sermon, "General Spread," ¶21.

28. Sermon, "General Spread," ¶22.

29. Sermon, "General Spread," ¶13–14.

30. Walter Huffman, "The Cost of Making Disciples," *Institute of Liturgical Studies Occasional Papers* (1996), 161–167.

31. Congregational worship has too often focused on celebrating the nature of God without reference to people or celebrating the accomplishments of people without reference to God. Rather, mission-shaped worship will celebrate the presence, work, and leading of God in our daily lives through testimony, praise, and prayer. And this will flow from gathering as smaller groups of disciples who exhort one another to pursue a deeper and more responsive walk with God in the world.

CHAPTER THREE

1. Covenant, §16.

2. Sermon, "The Scripture Way of Salvation," WJW 6. For the best summary of Wesley's soteriology as a way of holy love, see Kenneth Collins, *The Theology of John Wesley: Holy Love and the Shape of Grace* (Abingdon Press, 2007).

3. Sermon, "The Way to the Kingdom," WJW 5.

4. Sermon, "Spiritual Worship," ¶2, WJW 6. See Fred Sanders, *John Wesley on the Christian Life* (Crossway, 2013), 103–129.

5. Sermon, "Justification by Faith," §I.1, WJW 5.

6. Sermon, "Spiritual Worship," §III.1–10, WJW 6.

7. Sermon, "The New Birth," §I.2, WJW 6.

8. Sermon, "On Living Without God in the World," WJW 7.

9. Sermon, "The End of Christ's Coming," WJW 6.

10. Sermon, "The End of Christ's Coming," §I.7, WJW 6.

11. Sermon, "Awake Thou that Sleepest," §II.10, WJW 5.

12. Letter, "To Mr. John Trembath," 1755, WJW 12:289.

13. Wesley, "The Character of a Methodist," ¶8, WJW 8:376–385.

14. Wesley, "Character," ¶16.

15. Sermon, "The New Creation," ¶18, WJW 6.

16. See Howard Snyder, *Salvation Means Creation Healed: The Ecology of Sin and Grace* (Wipf & Stock, 2011).

17. See Philip Meadows, "Entering the Divine Embrace: Towards an Ancient-Future Wesleyan Theology of Evangelism," *Wesley and Methodist Studies*, 3 (2011), 3–30.

18. Robert Webber, *The Divine Embrace: Recovering the Passionate Spiritual Life* (Baker Books, 2006), 18.

19. Webber, *Divine Embrace*, 18.

20. Sermon, "New Birth," §II.2, §IV.3.

21. Sermon, "The Great Privilege of Those that are Born of God," §III.2, WJW 5.

22. Sermon, "New Birth," §II.4.

23. Sermon, "Great Privilege," §III.3.

24. See Mt 5:48; 2 Cor 7:1; Eph 4:13; Phil 3:12; Col 1:28; and 1 Jn 4:18.

25. Sermon, "On Working Out Our Own Salvation," §I.2, WJW 6.

26. Sermon, "On Working Out Our Own Salvation," §III.4.

27. Sermon, "The Scripture Way of Salvation," §III.10, WJW 6.

28. Sermon, "On Visiting the Sick," ¶1–2, WJW 7.

29. Sermon, "Of Evil Angels," §II:9, WJW 6.

30. See Philip Meadows, "Mission Spirituality in the Early Methodist Preachers," in Robert Webster (Ed), *Perfecting Perfection* (Pickwick, 2015), 103–129.

CHAPTER FOUR

1. Covenant, §1.

2. Wesley explained all this in his sermon "The New Birth," §II.3, WJW 6.

3. Rupert Davies, *Methodism* (Pelican Books, 1963), ch. 1.

4. See Lives. These appeared in the *Arminian Magazine* (1778–1811), which was latterly renamed the *Methodist Magazine*.

5. Philip Meadows, "Mission Spirituality in the Early Methodist Preachers," 112–113.

6. See Hymns, preface and table of contents. https://archive.org /details/collectionofhym00wesl (Accessed, June 2017).

7. Wesley, "Letter on Preaching Christ," WJW 11:575–576.

8. See Hymns, 1, 2, 75, 81, 83, 85, 109, 113, 118, 122, 124, 133.

9. See Hymns, 99, 100, 101, 110, 119, 121, 134, 137, 147.

10. See Philip Meadows, "Embodying Conversion," in Kenneth Collins & John Tyson (Ed.), *Conversion in the Wesleyan Tradition* (Abingdon Press, 2001).

11. Sermon, "The Means of Grace," §V.1, WJW 5.

12. Sermon, "The Means of Grace," §V.2–3.

13. Thomas Albin, "Finding God in Small Groups," *Christianity Today*, 47:8 (2003), 42–44.

14. See Treatise. Also John Wesley, *Thoughts Upon Infant Baptism* (John Mason, 1837).

15. Brian Brewer, "Evangelical Anglicanism: John Wesley's Dialectical Theology of Baptism," *Evangelical Quarterly*, 83:2 (2011), 107–132.

16. Wesley, "A Farther Appeal to Men of Reason and Religion," WJW 8:51–52.

17. Sermon, "The New Birth," §IV.4, WJW 6.

18. Treatise, §II.5.

19. Journal, 24 May 1738, WJW 1:114.

20. Sermon, "Marks of the New Birth," §IV.5, WJW 5.

21. Wesley, "Advice to the People Called Methodists," §VI.4, WJW 11:558.

22. Felton, *This Gift of Water*, ch. 3.

23. Henry Knight, "The Significance of Baptism for the Christian Life: Wesley's Pattern of Christian Initiation," *Worship* (1989), 136–138.

24. Hoyt Hickman, "The Role of Baptism in the Faith and Life of the United Methodist Church Today," *Perkins Journal* (Winter, 1981), 22–27.

25. Laurence Wood, "Methodism and the Recently Revised Baptismal Liturgy," *The Asbury Theological Journal*, 59 (2004), 233–238.

26. Spirituality, 99.

27. See L. Edward Phillips and Sara Webb Phillips, *Baptism: Understanding God's Gift* (Discipleship Resources, 2012).

28. Confirmation with water would not amount to rebaptism because infant baptism would not be viewed as complete in itself. Rather, infant baptism would be considered an authentic but incomplete sign of participation in the kingdom, anticipating fulfillment in the practice of believer's baptism.

29. St Thomas Philadelphia Church, *Preparing for Baptism* (Sheffield, 2012), 21.

30. Felton, *This Gift of Water*, 40.

CHAPTER FIVE

1. Covenant, §2.

2. Walter Brueggemann, *Biblical Perspectives in Evangelism* (Abingdon Press, 1993), 72–73.

3. From the perspective of Wesleyan theology, the Lord's Supper is a means of grace. We remember that Jesus is really present and open our hearts to his Spirit so we might be assured of forgiveness, filled with his strength, and sent out to fulfill his Great Commission.

4. J.I. Packer, *A Quest for Godliness: The Puritan Vision of the Christian Life* (Crossway, 2010), and Leland Ryken, *Worldly Saints: The Puritans as They Really Were* (Zondervan, 1990).

5. David Tripp, *The Renewal of the Covenant in the Methodist Tradition* (Epworth, 1968), and William Parkes, "Watchnight, Covenant Service, and the Love-Feast in early British Methodism," *Wesleyan Theological Journal*, 32:2 (1997), 35–58.

6. John Wesley, *Directions for Renewing Our Covenant with God*, 2nd Edition (1781). This can also be found in Frank Whaling, *John and Charles Wesley: Selected Writings and Hymns* (Paulist Press, 1981), 141–142. See Marion Jackson, "An Analysis of the Source of John Wesley's 'Directions for Renewing Our Covenant with God'," *Methodist History*, 30:3 (1992), 176–184.

7. Wesley, *Directions*, 19–20.

8. Wesley, *Directions*, 21.

9. Wesley, *Directions*, 21, 23.

10. Wesley, *Directions*, 17.

11. Wesley, *Directions*, 16.

12. Wesley, *Directions*, 3.

13. Wesley, *Directions*, 3.

14. Wesley, *Directions*, 4.

15. It was Jewish custom for the eldest son to bury his father in order to obtain his inheritance.

16. Wesley, *Directions*, 4.

17. Wesley, *Directions*, 4–5.

18. Sermon, "The Good Steward," WJW 6.

19. Wesley, *Directions*, 11.

20. Sermon, "Self Denial," ¶2, WJW 6.

21. Sermon, "Self Denial," §I.4.

22. Wesley, *Directions*, 12.

23. Wesley, *Directions*, 13.

24. Wesley, *Directions*, 14.

25. Wesley, *Directions*, 15.

CHAPTER SIX

1. Covenant, §6–8.

2. W.M. Reeves, *The Apology of Tertullian* (Newberry House, 1709), 56, ch.XVIII. http://www.tertullian.org/articles/reeve_apology.htm (Accessed, June 2016).

3. Alistair Stewart-Sykes, *Hippolytus: On the Apostolic Tradition: An English Version with Introduction and Commentary* (St. Vladimir's Seminary, 2001).

4. People, ¶10.

5. In what follows, I am especially indebted to Alan Kreider, *The Patient Ferment of the Early Church* (Baker Academic, 2016), and Robert Webber, *Journey to Jesus* (Abingdon, 2001).

6. Reeves, *Apology of Tertullian*, 143, §L.

7. D.M. Kay, *The Apology of Aristides the Philosopher* (Cambridge University Press, 1891). http://www.tertullian.org/fathers/aristides_00_title .htm (Accessed, June 2017).

8. Roberts-Donaldson (Tr.), *Didache*. http://www.earlychristian writings.com/text/didache-roberts.html (Accessed, June 2017).

9. Kreider, *Patient Ferment*, 133.

10. Reeves, *Apology of Tertullian*, 110, §XXXIX. See John 13:35.

11. See Daniel Benedict, *Come to the Waters* (Discipleship Resources, 1996), 9–10.

12. Rodney Stark, *The Rise of Christianity* (Harper, 1997), ch. 4.

13. When requiring people to give up their work, the early Christian community would support such persons materially and enable them to find other occupations.

14. Webber, *Journey to Jesus*, 97–99.

15. Kreider, *Patient Ferment*, 179.

16. Webber, *Journey to Jesus*, 168.

17. Raneiro Cantalamessa, *The Sober Intoxication of the Spirit* (Servant Books, 2005), 2.

18. Cantalamessa, *Sober Intoxication*, 3. See Acts 2:15, Eph 5:18.

19. People, ¶2. See also, Ted Campbell, *John Wesley and Christian Antiquity* (Kingswood Books, 1991).

20. People, §I.7.

21. Rules. Wesley drew the three principles from Is 1:16–17.

22. Sermon, "On Working Out Our Own Salvation," §II.4, WJW 6.

23. Rules, ¶3.

24. David Lowes Watson, *The Early Methodist Class Meeting: Its Origins and Significance* (Wipf & Stock, 2002), and D. Michael Henderson, *John Wesley's Class Meeting: A Model for Making Disciples* (Evangel Publishing House, 1997).

25. People, §II.7.

26. Wesley likened to the commendatory letters issued by the Apostles in Scripture. See 1 Cor 16:3; 2 Cor 3:1-3.

27. Sermon, "On God's Vineyard," §III.1–2, WJW 7.

28. See Philip Hardt, "The Evangelistic and Catechetical Role of the Class Meeting in Early New York Methodism," *Methodist History*, 38:1 (1999). See also, Tory Baucum, *Evangelical Hospitality: Catechetical Evangelism in the Early Church and Its Recovery for Today* (Scarecrow, 2008).

29. Rules, ¶5.

30. See Kevin Watson, *Pursuing Social Holiness: The Band Meeting in Wesley's Thought and Popular Methodist Practice* (Oxford University Press, 2015). For a contemporary innovation of the band meeting, see the Inspire Movement, https://inspiremovement.org/movement/vision/fellowship -bands (Accessed, June 2017).

31. Wesley, "Rules of the Band Societies," WJW 8:290–291.

32. People, §VI.3.

33. People, §VI.1.

34. People, §VI.6.

35. People, §VIII.1–3.

36. Spirituality, 74.

37. Sermon, "On Visiting the Sick," WJW 7.

38. Cited in John English, "Dear Sister:" John Wesley and the Women of Early Methodism, *Methodist History*, 33:1 (1994), 26.

39. People, §XI.4.

40. English, "Dear Sister," 30.

41. People, §XIII.3.

CHAPTER SEVEN

1. Covenant, §4.

2. C. Dodgson (Ed.), Tertullian Vol. 1, *Apologetic and Practical Treatises* (1842), 158–186, "The Crown."

3. Lorenzo Scupoli, *The Spiritual Combat* (Tan Books, 1990), 45–46.

4. Brueggemann, *Biblical Perspectives*, 19–25.

5. D. Dunn Wilson, *Many Waters Cannot Quench* (Epworth Press, 1969), 107–120.

6. Journal, 26 February 1767, WJW 3:262. See Wesley, "Character of a Methodist," WJW 8:376–385. This was inspired by Clement of Alexandria (150–215 AD). See David Bundy, "Christian Virtue: John Wesley and the Alexandrian Tradition," *Wesleyan Theological Journal*, 26 (1991), 139–163.

7. Sermon, "Satan's Devices," WJW 6.

8. Wesley, "Character," ¶5.

9. Wesley, "Character," ¶6–9. See 1 Thes 5:16-18.

10. See Lk 18:11; Heb 11:27; Jn 4:14; 1 Jn 4:18, and Phil 4:4, 11.

11. See Jn 14:21; Rom 12:1; Mt 5:8; 1 Jn 2:15; Gal 6:14; and Jn 6:38.

12. Wesley, "Character," ¶16. See Mk 12:33; 1 Jn 4:21.

13. Wesley, "Character," ¶17.

14. Wesley, "A Plain Account of Christian Perfection," ¶10, WJW 11:433.

15. Letter, "Second Letter to Lord Bishop of Exeter," ¶17, WJW 9:35. Also Journal, 26 Feb 1767, WJW 3:262–3.

16. See Philip Meadows, "The End of Discipleship: John Wesley's Vision of Real Christianity," in Tracy Cotterell & Mark Greene, *Imagine: The Disciple-Making Church* (Authentic, 2007).

17. Sermon, "Causes of the Inefficacy of Christianity," ¶7, WJW 7.

18. Sermon, "On Dissipation," WJW 6, and "On the Deceitfulness of the Human Heart," WJW 7.

19. Sermon, "On Dissipation," ¶15, 20.

20. Wesley identifies this general problem in his, "Letter on Preaching Christ," WJW 11:575–6.

21. Adam Clarke, *The Miscellaneous Works of Adam Clarke* (Tegg & Son, 1836), 257–8. Clarke recounts a personal conversation with his friend John Pool, to whom Whitefield had made this confession. https://archive.org/stream/04551794.445.emory.edu/04551794_445_djvu.txt. Accessed, 31 August 2017. There is some dispute about the accuracy of this account, but the point remains the same.

22. Journal, 25 August 1763, WJW 3:124.

23. Preface to Wesley, *Hymns and Sacred Poems* (1739), ¶5, WJW 14:437.

24. Preface to Wesley, *Hymns and Sacred Poems*, ¶6, WJW 14:438.

25. Wesley, *A Plain Account of the People Called Methodists*, §I.11.

26. Wesley, "A Plain Account of Christian Perfection," WJW 11:507.

27. Howard Snyder, *The Radical Wesley and Patterns for Church Renewal* (IVP, 1980), 2–4. Snyder got this term from Charles Ferguson, *Organizing to Beat the Devil: Methodists and the Making of America* (Doubleday, 1971). See also Joel B. Green and Mark Lau Branson, "Organize to Beat the Devil," *The Gospel and Our Culture Network*, 12:4 (2000), 1–5.

28. Sermon, "On God's Vineyard," §III.1, IV.1, WJW 7.

29. See Prayers. Originally 1733, and reprinted on at least seven occasions during Wesley's lifetime.

30. Willimon, *Remember Who You Are*, ch.9.

31. Notes, Rom 6:6, Eph 4:24.

32. Scupoli, *Spiritual Combat*, ch. 1. See 2 Cor 10:4.

33. Sermon, "The End of Christ's Coming," WJW 6. Based on 1 Jn 3:8.

34. Prayers, 238–239.

35. Prayers, 242.

36. Prayers, 253.

37. Prayers, 260.

38. Prayers, 266.

39. Prayers, 276.

40. See Laurence Stookey, *Baptism: Christ's Act in the Church*, 79f.

41. Treatise, §II.3.

42. Sermon, "The Mystery of Iniquity," ¶2–4, WJW 6.

43. Sermon, "Mystery of Iniquity," ¶32, 35.

44. Sermon, "On Obedience to Pastors," WJW 7. Hebrews 13:17.

45. Sermon, "Self Denial," §III.3, WJW 6.

46. I note that both the British Methodist Church and the Church of England have only a general renunciation of "evil," having removed the language of sin and spiritual warfare from their baptismal vows.

CHAPTER EIGHT

1. Covenant, §8.

2. Covenant, §1.

3. For example, Barry Callen, *Radical Christianity: The Believers Church Tradition in Christianity's History and Future* (Evangel, 1999).

4. See William Estep, *The Anabaptist Story*, 3rd Edition (Eerdmans, 1996).

5. Rodney Clapp, *A Peculiar People: The Church as Culture in a Post-Christian Society* (IVP, 1996), 99–102.

6. Howard Snyder, *The Radical Wesley and Patterns for Church Renewal* (IVP, 1980), 89.

7. See Stuart Murray, *Post-Christendom: Church and Mission in a Strange New World* (Paternoster, 2004).

8. For a critique of this approach, see Philip Kenneson and James Street, *Selling Out the Church: The Dangers of Church Marketing* (Cascade, 2003).

9. Alan Kreider, *The Change of Conversion and the Origin of Christendom* (Wipf & Stock, 2006), ch. 8. See also Murray, *Post-Christendom*, 200–206.

10. Stanley Hauerwas and William Willimon, *Resident Aliens: Life in the Christian Colony* (Abingdon Press, 1989), ch. 4.

11. See Graham Tomlin, *The Provocative Church* (SPCK, 2004).

12. Clapp, *A Peculiar People*, chs. 3, 5.

13. John Howard Yoder, *Body Politics: Five Practices of the Christian Community Before a Watching World* (Herald Press, 2001), ch. 6.

14. See Tod Bolsinger, *It Takes a Church to Raise a Christian* (Brazos Press, 2004).

15. Yoder, *Body Politics*, ch. 1. See Mt 18:6-9.

16. Yoder, *Body Politics*, 7–8.

17. John Wesley, *Sermons on Several Occasions* (Epworth Press, 1985).

18. Sermon, "Sermon on the Mount IV," WJW 5.

19. George Eli, *Social Holiness: John Wesley's Thinking on Christian Community and its Relationship to the Social Order* (Peter Lang, 1994), chs. 5, 6.

20. Sermon, "Of the Church," ¶15, 16, 20, WJW 6.

21. Sermon, "Of the Church," ¶30.

22. Bryan Stone, *Evangelism after Christendom: The Theology and Practice of Christian Witness* (Brazos Press, 2007), 118.

23. Sermon, "Of Former Times," ¶16, WJW 7. Also, Sermon, "The Mystery of Iniquity," ¶27–28, WJW 6.

24. Sermon, "Sermon on the Mount IV," §I,5, WJW 5.

25. Sermon, "Sermon on the Mount IV," §II.1, 2, 4.

26. Sermon, "On Friendship with the World," ¶1–7, WJW 6. Sermon, "Sermon on the Mount IV," §I.5.

27. Sermon, "In What Sense We Are to Leave the World," ¶9, 11, WJW 6. Also Sermon, "Friendship," ¶13f.

28. Sermon, "Friendship," ¶8–9.

29. Wesley, "Leave the World," ¶19.

30. Sermon, "On Family Religion," §I.2, WJW 7.

31. Sermon, "Family Religion," §III.12–18.

32. Sermon, "On Obedience to Parents," §I.7, 10; §II.4–5, WJW 7. Also Sermon, "On the Education of Children," ¶15, WJW 7. See Prov 22:6.

33. Rules, ¶7.

34. Philip Meadows, *Remembering Our Baptism*, Occasional Papers 97 (General Board of Higher Education and Ministry, 2001).

CHAPTER NINE

1. Covenant, §10.

2. Covenant, §11.

3. Hymns, 464.

4. Vinson Synan, *The Holiness–Pentecostal Tradition: Charismatic Movements in the Twentieth Century* (Eerdmans, 1997). Also Randall Stephens, "The Holiness/Pentecostal/Charismatic Extension of the Wesleyan Tradition" in Randy Maddox and Jason Vickers, *The Cambridge Companion to John Wesley* (Cambridge University Press, 2010).

5. See Frank Macchia, *Baptized in the Spirit: A Global Pentecostal Theology* (Zondervan, 2006) and Mark Cartledge, *Encountering the Spirit: The Charismatic Tradition* (Orbis Books, 2006).

6. Stephen Clark, *Charismatic Spirituality* (Servant Books, 2004), ch. 1.

7. William Arthur, *The Tongue of Fire: Or The True Power of Christianity* (Seedbed, 2015).

8. Max Turner, "Revival in the New Testament?" in Andrew Walker and Kristin Aune (Eds.), *On Revival: A Critical Examination* (Paternoster Press, 2003), 16–18.

9. For a lively description of the spiritual experience gifted through baptism in the Spirit, see Jurgen Moltmann, *The Source of Life* (Fortress Press, 1997).

10. Sermon, "The Great Privilege of Those That Are Born of God," WJW 5.

11. John Stott, *Baptism and Fullness: The Work of the Holy Spirit Today* (IVP, 2006), ch. 2.

12. Walker and Aune, *On Revival*, 1f.

13. Sermon, "The General Spread of the Gospel," ¶17, WJW 6.

14. See James Logan, *How Great a Flame: Contemporary Lessons from the Wesleyan Revival* (Discipleship Resources, 2005).

15. See Mark Stibbe, "Seized by the Power of a Great Affection," in Walker and Aune, *On Revival*, 23–42.

16. Herbert McGonigle, *The Methodist Pentecost: 1758–1763* (Moorley's, 2016). Also, Laurence Wood, *The Meaning of Pentecost in Early Methodism* (Scarecrow Press, 2002).

17. Journal, 28 October 162, WJW 3:95. Also Journal, 15 November 1763, WJW 3:138.

18. Wesley, "Brief Thoughts on Christian Perfection," ¶1, WJW 11:523.

19. Meadows, "Mission Spirituality in the Early Methodist Preachers," 114–120.

20. Lives, 6:186.

21. Spirituality, 92.

22. Journal, 29 February 1760, WJW 2:588; 25 December 1762, WJW 3:103; 1 January 1771, WJW 3:416.

23. Hymns, 473.

24. Wesley, "Directions for Congregational Singing," ¶5, WJW 14:466.

25. Preface to Hymns, ¶8, WJW 14:461.

26. Hymns, 363.

27. Hymns, 365.

28. See, for example, Journal, 19 July 1761, WJW 3:46.

29. Hymns, 506.

30. Minutes, 24.

31. Spirituality, 273–274.

32. Sermon, "The Means of Grace," §II.3, WJW 5.

33. Stuart Piggin, *Firestorm of the Lord* (Paternoster, 2000), ch. 4.

34. Charles Finney, *Lectures on Revivals of Religion* (1868), 11. http://www.ccel.org/ccel/finney/revivals.html (Accessed, June 2017).

35. Spirituality, 111–112.

36. Phoebe Palmer, *The Way of Holiness* (1854), §1, 17f. http://name.umdl.umich.edu/AJH1642.0001.001 (Accessed, June 2017).

37. Piggin, *Firestorm*, ch. 3.

38. See A.W. Tozer, *How to Be Filled with the Holy Spirit* (Moody, 2016), ch. 3.

CHAPTER TEN

1. Wesley, "Thoughts Upon Methodism," WJW 13:320.

2. George Hunter, *The Recovery of a Contagious Methodist Movement* (Nashville, TN: Abingdon, 2011) and Gil Rendle, *Back to Zero: The Search to Rediscover the Methodist Movement* (Nashville, TN: Abingdon, 2011). Both these books tend to focus on matters of structure rather than spirit.

3. This genome is developed further in Philip Meadows, *The Wesleyan DNA of Discipleship* (Grove Books, 2013). The fourfold genetic code of Wesleyan mission spirituality, outlined here, forms the "way of life" nurtured by the Inspire Movement. http://inspiremovement.org/movement /vision/ (Accessed, June 2017). Much of the theological reflection in this chapter has arisen from the author's involvement in this movement.

4. Letter, "To the Bishop of Bristol," 25 June 1746, WJW 12:97.

5. Letter, "To the Rev Mr. D_," 6 April 1761, WJW 12:303.

6. Scott Kisker, *Mainline or Methodist? Rediscovering Our Evangelistic Mission* (Discipleship Resources, 2008), ch. 1.

7. Steve Addison discusses the connections between white-hot faith, contagious relationships and adaptive methods in *Movements That Change the World*, Revised (IVP, 2011).

8. William Sangster, *Methodism: Her Unfinished Task* (Epworth, 1947) and *Methodism Can Be Born Again* (Hodder & Stoughton, 1938).

9. Wesley, *Plain Account of Christian Perfection* (1777), ¶1–5, WJW 14:428–429.

10. See Robert Tuttle, *Mysticism in the Wesleyan Tradition* (Zondervan, 1989).

11. Meadows, "Mission Spirituality in the Early Methodist Preachers," 116–117.

12. Lives, 1:152, 5:127, 6:176.

13. Sermon, "The Means of Grace," WJW 6.

14. Sermon, "The Scripture Way of Salvation," §III:10, WJW 6.

15. Sermon, "On Zeal," §II:9, WJW 7.

16. Sermon, "Upon Our Lord's Sermon on the Mount IV," §III.4, WJW 5.

17. Lives, 4:220, 5:160.

18. Sermon, "Sermon on the Mount IV," §III.1.

19. Sermon, "The Good Steward," WJW 6.

20. Prayers, Thursday Evening.

21. Sermon, "On Visiting the Sick," §II:2–4 & III:3, WJW 7.

22. Sermon, "Visiting the Sick," §III:5.

23. Lives, 5:257.

24. Lives, 3:85, 132.

25. Lives, 5:159–60.

26. People, §VIII:2.

27. See, http://www.umcdiscipleship.org/leadership-resources/covenant
-discipleship; and http://inspiremovement.org (Accessed, June 2017).

28. Sermon, "On Zeal."